IRISH LAW

FOR THE LAYPERSON

Judge us
by our
service

Any bank can lend you money. But not every bank
will give you our level of person-to-person service.
Whether you're looking for a loan to buy a house, a car
or a business premises why not talk to ACCBank.

For further details phone 1850 234 234 or your local branch.

Irish Law for
the Layperson

© **Michael A. O'Brien, B.C.L., Solicitor.**
ISBN 0 9529612 0 2

Editor: Patrick J. Ahern, B.C.L.

Typesetting: Fleming Graphics,
                 Mill Road, Midleton, Co. Cork.

Printing: GK Print, Grannagh, Waterford.

ACKNOWLEDGMENTS

I have received assistance from a number of people in the preparation of this book. In particular I should like to thank the following: The Editor Patrick J. Ahern, B.C.L., who also assisted in many other ways; Marguerite Bolger, B.L. who read a number of chapters of the book and made many helpful suggestions;

Vinóg Faughnan, B.L., for his assistance with the chapter on 'Succession Law'; Martin O'Sullivan, Co-Author of The Irish Farmers and Family Handbook, for his advice in a number of practical matters; and to all who work with me at Michael A. O'Brien and Company for their assistance throughout its preparation.

To the memory of my late father, Paul O'Brien.

AUTHOR'S NOTE

The law referred to in this book is the current law in the Irish Republic. I have endeavoured to state the law as it presently exists at the date of going to press. No responsibility or liability can be accepted for any omissions or errors contained in this book.

Its objective is to give the lay reader a general knowledge of the principles of Irish Law in a number of important areas. This is not a legal text book. There are a number of other aspects of Irish Law not dealt with in this publication such as Constitutional Law, Company Law and other specialised areas. There are many text books available which deal with these more specialised aspects of Irish Law

Michael A. O'Brien, 1st November, 1996.

CONTENTS

1 IRISH LEGAL SYSTEM

What is Law?

On the face of it this is an easy question to answer. Law is a set of rules. These rules are governed by principles. The principles in turn are influenced by concepts which come from policies or politics.

It is not difficult to discover what the rules are. It takes a trained lawyer to decide to what extent the rules match the principles. For the most part the legal rule is enough to tell us what to do.

In Ireland legal rules are contained in written laws called legislation or Acts of the Oireachtas. This accounts for about 5% of our law. The remainder is contained in written judgments of the Courts, particularly the High Court and Supreme Court. Again it takes a person trained in the law to find and understand the law fully with regard to any given circumstance.

To do this, solicitors and barristers like to pigeon-hole different areas of the law in order to help them to find and research it for their clients. In this book we have taken a selection of these areas and dealt with them individually.

These are areas of general concern that a Solicitor experiences year after year. Often they may overlap and a Solicitor could find several different issues in the same case.

Types of Law and their Order of Precedence

European Community Law

This is at the top of the scale and takes precedence over any other type of national law in the areas it effects; these include free movement of persons, goods, capital and finance in the E.U., employee protection and competition.

The Constitution

This is the supreme national law. It was first adopted in 1937 by a referendum and has been changed many times since.

Legislation

Another word for this is statute law. These are Acts of the Oireachtas formed by the Government of the day to cover any particular area of domestic or foreign policy. Another type of legislation is a Statutory Instrument or S.I. This is a regulation brought into effect by a Minister of a Government Department which may be needed immediately but the regulation must be within the terms of the parent Act. An example of this would be S.I. 266 of 1995 governing Milk Quota Regulations. S.I's like this are also used to bring in European Community Law regulations where need be, such as the example given. In a busy parliament such as our Dáil many different pieces of legislation are worked on and enacted each year to enhance the well-being and growth of our country and society in general.

Local authority bye-laws such as parking rules, water and refuse, rates, etc would be pitched at the same level as national legislation.

Judge Made Law

Strange as it may seem, judges do make law. In the course of justice judges must of necessity do so. Similarly in their interpretation of written legislation they do this also. This law is passed on in the form of written judgments and is contained in law reports, which are books available in law libraries. Traditionally, there are two different types of judge made law.

Equity

Another name for this is Chancery law. Formally the Chancellor and his aides were responsible for this. It is derived from the Church Courts which at one time were more powerful than any other. They acted as a type of appeal court where a person who might have a just case was unable to get it resolved by Common Law Courts.

Common Law

This derives its name from the law which was "common to all of England". After independence, the Dáil decided to keep the British common law system as a matter of expediency rather than attempt to revamp the whole thing and introduce a civil law system which is used on the continent today.

Common law is, along with Statutes, the most commonly used form of legal administration in Ireland today. Just because it is called 'common' does not mean that it is confined to the lower courts only. Indeed the Supreme Court in Ireland, The United States Federal Supreme Court and the House of Lords of the British legal system all use common law. Almost all litigation, criminal law, contract law etc is based in common law.

Constitutional Law

This is made when the High Court and Supreme Court interpret not just the plain meaning of the words of the Constitution but the implied or hidden meaning also.

The Constitution itself is divided into two main sections. The first defines and explains the Nation, the State and its Government. This is called administrative constitutional law. It is important when the citizen is dealing with the various branches of government, local authorities, Gárdai, etc to be aware of this.

The other part of the Constitution is the side that receives more high profile attention in referendums. It contains the personal rights of the citizens of Ireland and also covers the rights of non-citizens. These are both written, or express rights and implied, or hidden rights. Sometimes these rights take precedence (in other words are superior) to laws passed by government.

Precedent

Once a judgment has been made by a court the rule in that judgment must be followed in subsequent judgments on that same issue. An example in litigation occurred when someone was accidentally given food poisoning after drinking beer from a bottle containing a dead snail. The court held that even though there was no direct contact through the sale of the product between the producer and consumer, that injured person could still sue that producer. Translated into a rule this means that an injured party may obtain compensation from certain persons who cause them injury. This was then a precedent to be followed by other courts in the future.

In a national context precedent is handed down in the reports of the Supreme Court and High Court. It is usual for these courts, in the absence of our own native precedent to follow that of other common law jurisdictions or countries with similar legal systems, such as England, Canada, Australia or the United States.

The Irish Courts System

The main portion of this consists of the following in order of assent:

The District Court

Every town in Ireland has a District Court. It is presided over by one Judge. Each Judge is allocated a certain area in the country. Their work load is very heavy and consists of a variety of different types of work. It deals with both criminal matters and civil matters. This ranges from applications for bar extensions to preliminary hearings dealing with charges of murder, manslaughter, rape and other very serious crimes. It also hears preliminary enquiries into applications for extradition. The District Court has jurisdiction or authority to deal with cases involving sums up to £5,000. There could be any number of actions and would include actions for debt, breach of contract, or litigation resulting from accidents of various kinds.

The District Court also has authority to deal with many criminal matters such as drug offences, road traffic offences, assault and battery etc. It also has authority to deal with more serious offences where a person may choose to be tried in the District Court, for example larceny or stealing. It also receives appeals from certain tribunal hearings etc.

The Circuit Court

The Circuit Court has one Judge also. It 'sits' permanently in six main cities like Dublin, Cork. In other areas it goes "on circuit" to various provincial towns around the country.

The main types of civil cases with which the Circuit Court deals are cases arising from accidents known as personal injury actions, cases involving breaches of contract, cases involving nuisance or trespass, applications for injunctions and other types of civil cases. Serious criminal matters are also dealt with by the Circuit Court such as serious assaults, larceny, certain sexual offences, and other indictable offences. It acts as an appeal Court from the District Court and many decisions made by District Judges in the District Court are appealed to the Circuit Court on either of the grounds of the conviction itself or the penalty imposed. The Circuit Court has jurisdiction in civil cases from £5,000 up to £30,000. For a number of years there have been substantial delays in having civil cases heard in the Circuit Court of up to three years. However, a number of additional Judges have been appointed to the Circuit Court recently. The number of sittings of the Court have increased and it is hoped that the long delays and backlog will be cleared gradually.

Central Criminal Court

This Court deals with serious offences such as murder, attempted murder, offences under the Offences Against the State Act, 1939, Rape and other serious sexual offences. It comprises a Judge and Jury.

Court of Criminal Appeal

This Court hears appeals from the Circuit Court, the Central Criminal Court and the Special Criminal Court. It comprises three Judges. The Judges consider the transcript of evidence given at the original trial.

Special Criminal Court

This Court which is based in Dublin also consists of at least three Judges. It does not have a Jury. It deals with cases arising under the Offences Against the State Act which usually involve a subversive aspect.

The High Court

This deals with matters from a value of £30,000 with no upward limit. It acts as an appeal court from the Circuit Court and decides on points of law which are of exceptional legal importance from the District Court. It sits regularly in Dublin and goes on circuit during the year to the main provincial cities like Cork, Waterford, Limerick, Kilkenny, Galway, Sligo etc. Waiting lists are up to three years or more for an issue to go to trial. Legal and other costs can be very expensive and to be on the receiving end of a High Court action could be financially catastrophic, as usually the loser pays both sets of costs, as in any action.

The Supreme Court

This is the highest court in the land. It deals with appeals from the High Court. There are five Supreme Court judges and they have, like all judges, a very heavy work load. Coupled with this is the power to set the direction and tone of Irish society when they deliver their judgments.

The European Court of Justice

This Court sits in Luxembourg. Because Ireland is a member of the E.U., a certain amount of our law comes from there. The European Court of Justice is the court of the E.U.

Just because there is European law involved does not mean it must be attended to at the European Court of Justice. The Irish Courts can, and sometimes must, adjudicate on European Community law.

Children's Court

This forms part of the District Court where a District Judge deals with cases involving minor offences committed by children under the age of sixteen years. These cases are dealt with privately or "in camera" where only the Judge, the District Court Clerk and those representing the State and the Defence directly connected with the case are present.

The European Court of Human Rights and Fundamental Freedoms

This is another European Court. It is not to be confused with the European Court of Justice. The Court of Human Rights was set up after World War 2 to protect the Human Rights. It has nothing to do with the European Court of Justice or the E.U. Very few cases from the 50 or so member countries get to be heard before this court. It is confined to personal rights only which cannot be adequately decided by national law.

Court Officers

These are the Judges, the Barristers and Solicitors

Judges

Judges are appointed by the President. They are recruited from Barristers and Solicitors. At the moment Solicitors have access to judicial appointments in the District Court and Circuit Courts and also the High Court after they have served at least four years in the Circuit Court. Barristers have access to these also but can be appointed to the High Court and Supreme Court as well without any previous judicial experience.

To qualify, a barrister or solicitor must be appointed for at least ten years or twelve years for the High Court or Supreme Court. They forward their names to a panel of prospective appointees which is kept by the Judicial Appointments Committee. The committee assesses the applicants as to their qualification and suitability.

Judges, once they are appointed by the President of Ireland, cannot be removed or officially reprimanded by the government or anyone else.

Barristers

To become a Barrister a man or woman must pursue a long and strenuous course of education. They must be good at research and articulate at speech and debate.

The formal education consists of a primary university degree and a course at the Kings Inns in Dublin which is two years for law graduates and four years for non law graduates. This is a law school for barristers where they graduate with the degree of Barrister at Law, or B.L. They are then admitted to the list of barristers in Ireland by the Chief Justice of the Supreme Court. After this they do one year assisting an experienced barrister, known as 'devilling'.

The work of a barrister consists of advocating cases in court and the delivery of legal opinions. Much of the research and preparation for court is done by them in the law library situate in the Four Courts in Dublin. Junior Barristers are known as Junior Counsel. With adequate experience and a successful track record some Junior Counsel choose to become Senior Counsel. Senior Counsel conduct more advanced cases in the High and Supreme Court.

The wearing of wigs and black robes at one time was part of the dress code for barristers. Now the wig has become optional but many barristers choose to wear the it as it helps them remain anonymous in civilian life.

Solicitors

There are several ways to become a Solicitor. A person may have a primary degree from a university and sit the Incorporated Law Society entrance exam in eight legal subjects. By passing this and obtaining an apprenticeship with a practising solicitor of seven years standing that person may then be admitted to the roll of solicitors. An apprenticeship is two years long but with time added whilst waiting for a place in solicitors training school it may run into three or more years.

In order to become a Solicitor one has to go through a long and demanding training period. He or she will have acquired an extensive knowledge of the law and of all the different areas which will be encountered in practice. The Solicitor in practice will deal with a wide range of problems for his or her clients and while not a social worker or counsellor will assume the role of professional worrier for those clients. The qualified Solicitor will be well versed in the code of conduct and ethics of the profession.

Solicitors deal with a wide range of contentious issues and non-contentious issues for their clients. Much of the Solicitor's time is spent in the area of advising. He will also be a negotiator for his clients in endeavouring to resolve problems. Where problems cannot be resolved the Solicitor may institute Court proceedings or may be involved in defending Court proceedings. A detailed and careful preparation must be made by the Solicitor in preparing for a Court hearing. This will involve retaining a Barrister for hearings in higher courts, preparing all necessary documentation, serving the necessary documentation and notices on the opposing parties' Solicitor, making sure all the evidence is documented and ensuring that all relevant witnesses appear on the day of the hearing.

A great deal of the Solicitor's time is spent dealing with noncontentious issues. This may involve the drafting of legal documentation such as the documents required in the purchase or sale of property; drafting of Wills and other documents connected with the administration of estates. Also the preparation of mortgages and commercial leases and a broad range of legal agreements takes up a very large amount of the Solicitor's time.

Whereas many Solicitors work in general practice a number of Solicitors also work on an in-house basis in companies or Banks or other institutions. Whereas many Solicitors practice as general practitioners a number of Solicitors decide to specialise in particular areas of the law, e.g. commercial law, criminal law, conveyancing or litigation.

Contentious Issues

These are where a dispute exists between two or more individuals which is to be resolved either by negotiation or if this cannot resolve it, by a Judge in a Court.

When a Solicitor is preparing for a trial he or she must:

(i)   inform and instruct a Barrister

(ii)   prepare all the documents which must be filed in court

(iii)   serve the opposing party's solicitor with notices and documents

(iv)   make sure all the evidence is documented and ready

(v)   ensure that all witnesses are ready and appear on the day of the court.

Non Contentious Issues

Among these is the transfer of land and property...

When a person owns such property or realty (real estate) that person's name is on the deeds. A solicitor is the only person who is allowed by law to transfer a person's ownership.

Other non contentious work undertaken would be the drawing up of wills, mortgages, and leases. Indeed a substantial amount of the solicitor's work is in this area.

2 MARRIAGE AND THE LAW

Introduction

No other single area of the law has made the headlines in recent times. Family law, or more specifically for our purposes, marriage and the law is used to describe, amongst other things, the formation of marriage, separation, nullity, conciliation, judicial separation, divorce and all rights and entitlements which accompany them. Family law in general, is the area of most change in law in Ireland in many years. The creation of a separate department in the Government called the Department of Equality and Law Reform under Minister Mervyn Taylor has assisted in this to a large degree. There is no way a single chapter in any book could explain all there is to know about the law of marriage (or any other legal area for that matter). However an attempt to outline the main aspects which may be of interest to the lay reader should provide some interesting reading.

The Formation of a Marriage

For most Irish people marriage means a Church ceremony, a reception, honeymoon and a happy ever after life. This is, for all concerned, a most desirable situation. Very few people question what actually happens during a marriage service. They would rightfully think that love would keep them together. But there is, after the other binding forces such as religious, social and moral, a legal obligation which commences with a marriage service. When all the other obligations are removed by the parties themselves, this last one requires the intervention of the courts to undo that which has been put in place by the wedding ceremony. For a marriage to be legal, certain formalities need to be observed. The parties must be at least 18 years of age. They may be permitted to marry under that age but would require permission from the Circuit Court to do so. The wedding would need to take place in a registered building such as a Church, Synagogue or Registry Office. The parties would need to inform the Registrar of Marriages for their area at least three months in advance. The ceremony, to be valid, would need to be carried out in the presence of an ordained priest or minister or some other person duly appointed. They are required to sign the register and have their signatures witnessed by at least one person. Many of these, and other formalities, are often performed for example by the priest or other minister and do not occupy the full attention of the bride and groom. It may be of interest to note that even though the law places emphasis on these formalities, the lack of many of them will not invalidate a marriage. An example of this would be the requirement that the doors of the building be kept open during the ceremony.

What is a Marriage by Law?
A marriage is a legally binding contract where the terms of that agreement or contract involve the voluntary union of

a   one man and one woman

b   who promise to live together

c   to the exclusion of all

d   for life

This definition is broken down in order for us to examine it more closely.

"One Man and One Woman"
This begs the question - what about homosexual weddings which are now legal in some parts of the United States. In Ireland such a marriage would be deemed invalid as to the requirement of one of either gender.

Similarly multiple marriages where a man marries more than one wife, the other still living at the time of the second marriage. The second marriage would be invalid in law. The persons involved could be liable to criminal proceedings for bigamy.

Another issue raised here is that of a partner who undertakes a sex change operation and marries. Such cases have been handled by the courts who found that a person's sex is fixed at birth. Therefore, should a man undergo a sex change operation and become a woman, that person is still a man in the eyes of the law.

"The Promise to Live Together"

This was the requirement under the old legal definition. Today it is morally binding only but does have implications for desertion which provides grounds for divorce proceedings.

"Exclusion of All"

While we have mentioned that a bigamous marriage would be null and void in law we did not discuss the other type of extra-marital liaison. Adultery once proven can have serious results. Firstly the third party involved in an affair with a married person could be at risk from a civil action for damages brought by the offended partner in marriage. A famous example from history was that of the civil action brought by Captain O'Shea against Charles Stuart Parnell who had an affair with O'Shea's wife Kitty.

Another and often more serious affect of adultery is the ground it provides for judicial separation or divorce proceedings. As we shall see this can have devastating results in terms of family and material possessions.

"For Life"

The traditional and still the official description for marriage is that it is a lifetime commitment. When people make the vows (agree the terms) it is expected that they do not enter into it expecting to be divorced or judicially separated. For this reason the life time promise is presumed to apply.

The Two Functions of a
Priest or Minister

When a couple enter into a marriage they often use a religious service to do so. Church weddings are still as popular as they ever were. In Ireland most marriages are Roman Catholic, but the rules broadly apply to other denominations also. For the purposes of explanation it is most convenient to use the Roman model.

The priest in a marriage service performs two functions. Firstly he marries people in the eyes of God, according to the rites of the Church. Secondly he performs the function of a clerk of the Registry Office, and by his presence he fulfils a legal function which the couple require by law as they perform their contractual agreement. It is confusing and not quite accurate to say that the priest marries the couple. They marry each other. Priests satisfy the above requirements and are to be commended for their services to the community in this.

After the ceremony the priest attends to the signing of the register and ensures that it is witnessed by two people. One witness is enough to satisfy the law. The couple are then married and exist from that moment on in that state. They are legally bound to each other by the contract they have agreed.

Confusing Results

To most people in their everyday lives the law is at most a side issue. It is little surprise that a number of people do not fully appreciate the legal effects of marriage. Coupled with this is the more obvious element of a religious service which tends to down play the legal aspect. A good example of confusion in this occurred in the 1970's. Roman Catholic marriages in Lourdes required a separate French State registered service to validate them. Many Irish couples got married in the Church of Lourdes only and did not complete the State requirement. As a result these marriages were not valid in law in Ireland. When this phenomenon was discovered the Dáil rushed through an emergency law to correct it.

Conflict of Formalities Between the Roman Catholic Church and the State

There are some occasions where the Church's version of marriage does not match that of the State.

A marriage between two Roman Catholics before a priest but where no witnesses are available is a valid civil marriage. It is not valid in the eyes of the Church, however.

A registry office marriage only is not valid in the eyes of the Church. It was not unknown in the past for a person to marry in a registry office, then marry a second person in the Church with a priest present, and later be convicted of bigamy.

A person convicted of bigamy can be jailed for up to seven years. Any person who knows of the circumstances of the bigamist can be likewise convicted. This could include the second partner, the priest or witnesses.

Dissolution and Separation

We have discussed the formation of marriage from a legal viewpoint. The dissolution, on the other hand, of the partnership by legal means brings home the full extent of the input of the law's bearing on the formation of marriage. In order for married partners to go their separate ways, or at least suspend or cancel their relationships this requires use of the legal system. Of course for poor people, people with no assets, the solution is much simpler. Desertion was known as "the poor man's divorce". This does not solve the legal reality of the marriage remaining as it was formed. It can be of extreme comfort to know that one's relationship is above board, valid in the eyes of society and of the law, and that one's children will grow up in the security and comfort of their parents relationship which is understood by law. This is what motivates people to marry. It also moves them to go about divorce or nullity proceedings in order to clear the way for remarriage. Separation on the other hand is the usual method of dividing the shared assets, e.g. the family home, lifestyle, bank accounts etc. without the desire to remarry. There are two types of dissolution, i.e. nullity and separation and in turn separation can by Separation Agreement or by way of Judicial Separation or Divorce following the recent referendum.

Nullity

Nullity means the marriage never existed due to a defect or fault in one or both partners at the time of formation. This defect has as a legal consequence, i.e. the non event of the legal relationship. There are two types of marriages in this category. Void and voidable. Void means the marriage never existed. Any person who would be held to have any interest in such a marriage, e.g. parent, guardian or partner, etc. could apply to the court for a decree of nullity. A voidable marriage on the other hand means a valid existing marriage up to the time a decree is granted to an applicant. This occurs when a court decides that a marriage was flawed in its formation by a defect.

Defects

What are all these defects which seem to play such an important part in nullity?

The courts through the years have recognised some of the following, although new defects still arise from time to time.

Impotence

The marriage is voidable if either man or woman are unable to perform full sexual intercourse. Partial sexual intercourse by the male may be enough as emission is not a legal requirement. The defect must be present at the time of the marriage. Psychological impotence vis a vis one particular person or wilful refusal will provide valid grounds for a decree of nullity.

A person may rely on their own impotence and use this as grounds for a nullity.

Inability to enter into and sustain a normal marital relationship
This is a very broad category and includes marriages where a partner is incapable through illness of forming a caring or considerate relationship.

Many different types of psychiatric illnesses fall into this category. Again it is important that it is proven to the court's satisfaction that the illness was present during the formation of the marriage.

Personality disorders which can be proved to have existed by psychological testing, e.g. severe immaturity may be a valid ground for nullity. For example, the woman who married because she felt embarrassed at having a child outside wedlock, was found to have been spoiled, and unprepared to accept the obligations of marriage. This does not mean that every case of people who married because of pregnancy will have grounds for an annulment. The wide category of possible grounds are typified in this example. It is best should a person feel that they wish to obtain nullity of their marriage to see a Solicitor who would evaluate their case.

Homosexual Orientation
If a person is by reason of their homosexuality, incapable of entering into and sustaining a normal marital relationship, the other party may be entitled to an annulment. Again this is not necessarily viewed as any type of disorder. If a person is engaged in homosexual acts prior to the marriage but refrained from doing so afterwards, and lived in marriage in a heterosexual way, it would not then provide adequate grounds for nullity. This

person would have the capacity to enter into and sustain a normal marital relationship.

Normal Marriage

What is normal is a very hard standard to define. Relying on this ground for an annulment a person would have a hit or miss change of success. Much of the time the issues would be decided on expert evidence and may come down to this.

1. Is it clear that a continuation by the two parties of their relationship has become impossible?
2. Is it because of a scientifically usually psychiatrically, recognised incapacity in one of the parties?

If one partner in a marriage is relying on the above grounds, i.e. that of their own incapacity, they have to prove the other partner rejected the marriage.

Consent

The reader will remember our earlier description of marriage they will notice that it is a voluntary union. This means no valid marriage can take place where consent is missing to such a degree that one or both parties do not in their own minds volunteer or commit themselves gladly to the ceremony.

A person may be unable to consent either through infirmity of mind from a defect of reason or lack of sanity. However it is worth noting that the right to marry is a personal right under the Constitution and may be superior in standing to laws that say otherwise.

Other reasons which may invalidate a marriage is if a person is drunk at the time of marriage or on drugs. Again if a person wishes to use many of the grounds for nullity they should act as soon after the wedding as possible. Otherwise approbation might have an effect.

Duress and Pressurisation

What may be obvious to an onlooker might not reflect the true situation. A person can think they are in a situation in which they are not; they may be led to believe something which is untrue, or they might enter marriage for the wrong reason. All or any of these could fundamentally undermine a marriage. The test for this is whether that person, with regard to their personality, was overcome by pressure and were forced to marry. The types of pressure would include fear of threats, intimidation, trickery or brow beating.

Approbation

This occurs where even though a marriage may be fundamentally flawed and potentially invalid or indeed invalid but because the parties lived as a normal couple for some years afterwards the marriage may be held to be valid.

Pregnancy as a result of sexual intercourse before the marriage, if the primary reason for marriage, if not the desire for a relationship, as described earlier, may be a ground for nullity but will depend on the circumstances and the type of pressure put on the parties to marry.

Emotional pressure from parents, priest, relations or from one partner on another who may not be of a strong personality is also a ground. Similarly, emotional bondage which overcomes a person's rational thinking has been used to annul a marriage in recent times.

To take advantage of pressurisation however, it must first be established. A conspiracy between the parties, or collusion, if proved will destroy any chance of gaining the nullity. Collusion would be where both parties agree that the best thing would be to marry for the sake of appearances. This, as the reader will agree, is not duress or parental pressure.

Much of the time the courts will judge the personality of the person claiming the nullity in such cases. Where a strong or self-willed woman who was pregnant at marriage seeks a nullity she would find it more difficult than a meek and timid young girl in the same circumstances.

Other Reasons Why a Marriage will be Null and Void

a   A marriage between people where one is already validly married to a living person.

b   Homosexual or same sex marriages.

c   Foreign marriages which are celebrated

    1   without complying fully with that country's laws.

    2   and where foreign marriages in general are for fundamental reasons in conflict with Irish legal standards, e.g. polygamy, or are potentially so.

d   Prohibited degrees. These are marriages between full blood or half-blood relatives. They are void. Again this means anyone with an interest in such a marriage can petition a court for a decree of nullity.

The existing prohibited degrees are as follows:

A man may not marry his	A woman may not marry her
1. Grandmother	1. Grandfather
2. Grandfather's wife	2. Grandmother's husband
3. Wife's grandmother	3. Husband's grandfather
4. Father's sister	4. Mother's brother
5. Mother's sister	5. Mother's brother
6. Father's brother's wife	6. Father's sister's husband
7. Mother's brother's wife	7. Mother's sister's husband
8. Wife's father's sister	8. Husband' father's brother
9. Wife's mother's sister	9. Husband's mother's brother
10. Mother	10. Father
11. Stepmother	11. Stepfather
12. Wife's mother	12. Husband's father
13. Daughter	13. Son
14. Wife's daughter	14. Husband's son
15. Son's wife	15. Daughter's husband
16. Sister	16. Brother
17. Son's daughter	17. Son's son
18. Daughter's daughter	18. Daughter's son
19. Son's son's wife	19. Son's daughter's husband
20. Daughter's son's wife	20. Daughter's daughter's husband
21. Wife's son's daughter	21. Husband's son's son
22. Wife's daughter's daughter	22. Husband's daughter's son
23. Brother's daughter	23. Brother's son
24. Sister's daughter	24. Sister's son
25. Brother's son's wife	25. Brother's daughter's husband
26. Sister's son's wife	26. Sister's daughter's husband
27. Wife's brother's daughter	27. Husband's brother's son
28. Wife's sister's daughter	28. Husband's sister's son.

First cousins fall outside the prohibited degrees as above and may marry. Roman Catholic Canon law however requires permission from the Church.

Other prohibited degrees as above where non-blood relatives are involved are illegal as a matter of policy. Permission from the courts may be required before such marriages take place.

Effects of a Nullity Decree

A nullity decree could bestow several advantages, depending on a person's circumstances.

Advantages

If a marriage is annulled that means it never existed. If it never existed no rights to the spouses arise because of it. The practical effect of this is that ancillary orders which would be the normal part of divorce or judicial separation proceedings do not apply. These are powers that a court can use when deciding who gets what when a marriage is dissolved. The decision is based on evidence of income and assets. In a nullity situation the court will not undo any arrangements made between the parties and will not return to the individuals their own property where such arrangements were made on the assumption that the marriage was valid. So if a husband and wife own a house in both names under these circumstances, it will remain so after a nullity decree. The person that contributed to the purchase of the house will have to get an order from the High Court to get the ownership changed to their name. But orders on pension rights, assets, lump sum payments, orders for the sale of the family home, the extinguishment and restructuring of succession rights etc are not granted in nullity proceedings.

When the marriage is void, the parties are entitled to remarry without first obtaining a nullity decree from the court. It is wise to check this situation beforehand to ensure that the marriage does fall into this category. If it is merely voidable another marriage would be considered bigamous. However the obtaining of a nullity decree would then validate that second marriage.

Disadvantages

The children of a marriage which has been annulled are technically illegitimate. Since the Status of Children Act 1987 however non-marital children have been placed on a more equal footing, and recent constitutional developments have given fathers more access to such children. However, unlike other unmarried fathers who must apply to Court to be appointed guardians of their children, a father whose marriage to the mother has been annulled will have automatic guardian-ship rights over the children.

The down side is that nullity is more difficult to get, the grounds for which are much less than those of divorce.

Traditionally, nullity cases were heard in the High Court. This could be an expensive process for the people concerned. Now they can take place in the Circuit Court which makes them much more accessible in terms of cost.

It should be clearly understood that a Church Annulment is an entirely separate matter to a state annulment. Neither a church annulment or state annulment have any legal effect on either of the institutions. Therefore a person who succeeds in getting a state annulment may have to apply to the Church for an annulment before a religious ceremony can take place.

Separation Agreement

Where a marriage breaks down a husband or a wife may be advised to enter into a Separation Agreement to settle the terms of the marriage break up. This has the disadvantage of not giving the parties the right to remarry. However, if this procedure can bring about a satisfactory result it is generally far less expensive then the process of a Court hearing. It is usual for one of the Solicitors to write to the other party setting out the proposed terms of the Separation Agreement. The matters normally dealt with in a Separation Agreement are provision that the parties will live separate lives, custody and access of any children, maintenance, provisions regarding the family home, succession rights, taxation considerations and any other matters which may be relevant in the particular case.

Divorce and Judicial Separation

Introduction

Divorce is the dissolution of an otherwise valid and existing marriage. To get a divorce a person must fall into one of the categories, the structure of which were outlined, voted upon and passed by a very narrow margin during the referendum of 1995.

In order to give the reader some idea and to simplify divorce we outline below the main headings of the government's information paper on the right to remarry. It must be pointed out that since the Judicial Separation and Family Law Reform Act in 1989 there have been about 10,000 applications for judicial separation.

Family Mediation Service

This is a service which offers a couple a cheap and efficient method of going their separate ways. It involves a negotiated agreement and deals with matters such as maintenance, the division of property, the custody of, and access, to their children, if any, all with the help of a qualified counsellor. This service has operated since 1986 and is provided free of charge. This service is only available at present in Dublin and it is the Family Mediation Service, Block One, Fifth Floor, Irish Life Centre, Lower Abbey Street, Dublin 1.

Marriage Counselling
Unlike the family mediation service which sometimes helps couples who have decided to separate on an amicable basis, marriage counselling services aim to help couples with problems at the earlier stages. Its purpose is to prevent, if possible, a final breakdown.

Both the mediation and counselling services are operated with the assistance of government funding. The Marriage Counselling Service is situated at 24 Grafton Street, Dublin 2. The Catholic Marriage Advisory Council is at All Hallows College, Drumcondra, Dublin 9.

Judicial Separation

Prior to the introduction of divorce legislation this was the other main alternative. It still has its uses. These are many and varied and amongst others, those who through religious or moral objections do not see divorce as a favourable alternative. In addition it provides a way of deciding pressing issues such as maintenance, custody and property division at a stage when the parties have not been living apart long enough to be able to apply for a divorce.

The main effect of a judicial separation is that it removes the duty on the spouses to co-habit. There are six grounds on which a judicial separation may be granted. These are:

1.   Adultery

This involves by definition sexual penetration between persons of the opposite sex, one of whom is married. Otherwise it is not legal adultery. It does not have to be witnessed to prove it. It can be judged to have happened from the surrounding circumstances.

2.   Behaviour

In a nutshell, this is a valid ground if the party applying for the judicial separation shows a court that he or she cannot reasonably be expected to live with the other party, with regard to that persons behaviour. The intention of the offending party is irrelevant. This usually involves issues such as physical and/or emotional abuse.

3.   Desertion

An application to the courts may qualify if there has been desertion by the offending party for a continuous period of at least one year, prior to the date of the application. Similarly, a person can be driven out of their home by the attitude of the other. This is called "constructive desertion".

4.   Living apart for one year.

This allows the couple to agree on an amicable settlement and avoid the "mud-slinging" of a court battle. However in many cases this ground may not be available as a couple may continue to occupy the family home together for financial reasons or because they cannot decide who should move out. It has been held in some cases that one house has been changed into two households, thus making this ground available, but this will depend on the circumstances.

5.   No normal marital relationship for one year.

The big question here is what is "normal"? If the court finds that in all the circumstances that no normal relationship has existed it will grant the separation. Usually the Court will grant a separation on this ground where the parties have not had sexual relations for at least one year prior to the date of the application.

6.   Living apart for three years.

The difference here between the "one year apart" requirement and this is that a spouse who has been responsible for the breakdown in marriage may themselves apply, under the heading even against the wishes of the offending spouse.

Reconciliation

Under the 1989 Act, a solicitor, before he or she can take a case for a client must follow a schedule which attempts to reconcile the parties to a troubled marriage. This would include the provision of the names and addresses of mediation service centres.

What happens when a judicial separation decree is granted?

1. Parties are no longer legally obliged to live together. This has been unenforceable for years.
2. It clarifies the parties status.
3. It makes available a range of ancillary orders relating to custody, access, property and financial affairs, amongst others.

Ancillary Orders

These cover a range of orders which are made by a Judge. They are based on the evidence produced to him or her by the parties. Judges strive to strike a fair balance between the parties taking into account, amongst other things, the care and custody of the children if any and the financial dependence or otherwise of one spouse on the other.

The types of order are:-

1. Secured periodical payments. These are regular payments from one party to the other.
2. Lump sum orders. These can be a single payment of a lump sum or occasional payments of such. These may be to a spouse or a dependent child.

3. Property adjustment order. A court may order the transfer of any property from one spouse to another. It does not mean automatically transferring half the house of half the farm. It can also vary settlement, that is agreements outside the instant proceedings) and could include post or ante nuptial agreements or agreements which arise after a will has been executed.
4. An order relating to the family home.
    This could be for the occupancy of the family home for the life of one spouse or until a dependent child has reached a certain age or educational stage or the sale of the family home.
5. Extinguish succession rights. A court has the power to re-arrange a spouses will in favour of the other spouse or children and extinguish a legal right share of a spouse otherwise arising by law. (see the chapter on Succession).
6. Rearrangement of Pension Rights.

Divorce

Following the yes vote to the divorce referendum introducing divorce the Divorce Bill 1996 has now been drafted and is being considered.

The Constitution allows for divorce under the following

1. At the date of the institution of proceedings a couple who lived apart from one another for a period of, or periods amounting to, at least four years during the previous five years.
2. There is no reasonable prospect of reconciliation.

3. Proper provision having regard to the circumstances exists or has been made for the spouses and any dependent members of the family, and

4. Any other condition prescribed by law has been complied with.

If a person procures a decree of divorce they are free to marry again. This is the difference between divorce and judicial separation.

Either the Circuit Court or the High Court has jurisdiction or can hear cases of this nature. All cases as indeed all family law cases are heard "in camera". This means that no members of the press or public will be allowed to attend. Judges and Barristers will not wear wigs or gowns, which are normally optional to them.

A spouse may apply for a divorce where the other spouse has applied for judicial separation, or a decree of nullity. Once an application for divorce is made a court may make preliminary orders before a hearing. These can include maintenance orders, orders for the protection of spouses and children and orders to deal with protection of the family home.

After a decree of divorce has been granted a court can make orders similar to the ancillary orders given on the granting of a decree of judicial separation.

Conclusion

In the future we can expect to see a special division of the court system which deals with family law alone. At present the family law court is attached to the ordinary civil law courts which hears cases on all the other everyday matters. This is inconvenient for the parties involved as they often may have to share the same waiting rooms (if any) and are mixed in with the other litigants while awaiting their hearing.

There are already a large number of judicial separation cases pending before the Courts. The sittings of these Courts are much too infrequent for the volume of work to be dealt with. It is anticipated that when the system is introduced allowing for divorce to be applied for there will be a large volume of cases to be dealt with.

3 BUYING PROPERTY

Introduction

This is probably the single largest purchase in most peoples' lifetime. People need to contact their Solicitor on this occasion but some may say that they do not see the need to spend money on legal and other fees when they do not see what is being done for them. On completion of this chapter the reader will have a better insight into what occurs when they buy or sell a house, a farm or other property.

In this chapter, we look at the many different tasks which must be carried out when property is either sold or bought. Before a property transaction is completed there are many questions raised by the purchaser's Solicitor which need to be answered to ensure that the purchaser gets a good trouble free title to be registered.

Similarly, the Solicitor for the seller must ensure that the purchaser honours the agreement and that the agreed purchase price is paid and that the agreed completion date is honoured.

Title - Two Types

There are two types of title in Ireland known as Land Registry title and Registry of Deeds (unregistered) title. Land Registry title is that which is registered in a register maintained by the Land Registry. The owner of the property which is registered in the Land Registry will have a numbered folio. This document records the name and address of the owner, a description and particulars of the property and a map of the property known as a file plan. A folio is conclusive evidence of the person's ownership of the property. When one is selling Land Registry property one must produce a copy of the folio to establish the right to sell.

Registry of Deeds title is that which is registered in the Registry of Deeds. This occurs where the title has built up over a number of years. These documents would include Deeds of Conveyance used to transfer freehold unregistered land or Deed of Assignment used to transfer leasehold unregistered land.

On completion of a sale of unregistered property the purchase deed is lodged in the Registry of Deeds where the details of the registration and the time of the registration are noted on the Deed. The main reason for registering deed in the Registry of Deeds is that the time of registration governs conflicts between two different deeds, e.g if two mortgages on the one property are lodged on the one day the one which is registered first will gain priority over the one which is registered later.

Purchasing Property Procedures Outlined

Many of the procedures are standardised today. When an agreement has been reached the seller or the auctioneer for the seller will ask the seller's Solicitor to prepare a contract and send it to the purchaser's Solicitor. The contract together with the title will be sent by the seller's Solicitor to the purchaser's Solicitor who will then examine the contract and title thoroughly. There may be preliminary enquiries to be carried out in relation to matters contained in the contract. Having discussed the contract fully with the purchaser and after discussions with the seller there may be certain changes to be made in it. This entire process can take some time. Later we will look at the subject matter of the contract under a separate heading.

When all matters have been explained by the purchaser's Solicitor and if the purchaser is happy with the contract he will then sign it and pay a deposit which is usually ten per cent of the purchase price. There will usually be certain "special conditions" governing such matters as loan approvals or planning permissions or other matters.

If a loan is being obtained the contract will be made subject to the purchaser obtaining the loan. If the loan is not obtained the contract will be cancelled and the deposit returned. Similarly if a site is being bought and planning permission is being obtained a special condition will be inserted allowing the purchaser a specified time to obtain planning and ensuring that if planning is not obtained the deposit will be returned.

The purchaser's Solicitor will then raise a series of detailed questions relating to physical and legal matters relating to the property. These are known as Requisitions on Title. The Deed proposed to be signed by the parties is drafted and the contract deposit, draft Deed and requisitions are sent to the seller's Solicitor. A binding contract does not take place until the seller returns the contract signed, to the purchaser.

The seller's Solicitor will return the Requisitions on Title with the replies to all of the questions raised. Apart from legal questions regarding the title the Requisitions on Title will raise questions regarding matters such as planning permission and bye-lay approval, whether there are any unauthorised structures on the premises, boundaries, rights-of-way, and all other relevant questions relating to the physical aspects of the property.

After the Requisitions on Title have been replied to the seller's Solicitor hands over to the purchaser's Solicitor all the title documents and other documentation agreed, the keys and the purchase deed signed by the seller. The purchaser's solicitor hands over the balance of the purchase money.The matter is then completed as far as the seller is concerned subject to any undertakings given by his Solicitor – for example usually a mortgage will be paid off and the seller's Solicitor will undertake to pay same out of the proceeds of the sale, have the mortgage cancelled by the lending institution and have this then forwarded to the purchaser's Solicitor.

The purchaser's Solicitor after completion will have to carry out further work to finalise the registration of the purchasers ownership. This will include the stamping and registering of the purchase deed. Stamp duty is dealt with later in this chapter. The rule is that the document must be stamped within 28 days of signing as otherwise onerous penalties are imposed by the Revenue Commissioners.

After stamping the documentation is sent either to the Land Registry or the Registry of Deeds for registration and forwarded to the lending institution who holds the deed until the mortgage is paid off.

Contract

Irish law provides that the contract for sale must be in writing. The entire area of contract law is a very complex one. There are a large number of cases relation to disputes arising under the Law of Contract. The law provides that there must be evidence of a contract in writing maintaining the particulars of the transaction, the purchase price, the description of the property and identity of the parties involved. However the contract now used is the "Law Society Standard Form of Particulars and Conditions of Sale". This contract sets out the following:

1. The names and addressed of the parties to the transactions
2. The purchase price.
3. The deposit
4. The closing date.
5. The interest rate charged as a penalty where the purchaser fails to complete on the agreed closing date.
6. A full description of the property usually by reference to a map attached to the contract.
7. A full list of the documents being given by the seller to prove title to the property.

Title Documents

The deed used where Land Registry property sold is known as a Deed of Transfer. The Deed used to transfer freehold unregistered property is called a Deed of Conveyance. The Deed used to transfer leasehold on unregistered land is called a Deed of Assignment. A Deed of Mortgage is used to transfer the title to the lending institution during the term of the mortgage. All of these documents must be drawn up correctly. Depending on the title involved the drafting of these documents can be quite complicated. At the end to the day the Land Registry or Registry of Deeds must be satisfied that all the documentation is in order before they will register the ownership of a new purchaser.

Financial Planning

Even before choosing a property it would be extremely worthwhile for the purchaser's Solicitor to be consulted regarding financial implications of the proposed transaction. Matters which could be usefully discussed are:

a)   what the realistic price range for the house should be?

b)   how much should realistically be borrowed?

c)   how much would realistically be loaned by a lending institution given the salary of the borrower and/or the borrower's spouse? Lending institution will generally lend a particular multiple of the borrower's salary and will take the borrower's spouse's salary into account.

d)   what is the most favourable mortgage?

e)   what are the costs and expenses likely to amount to?

The solicitor's fee, registration fees payable to the Land Registry or Registry of Deeds, search fees, mortgage protection and fire insurance and in many cases the most significant cost item that is Stamp Duty are all major items for consideration.

Mortgages and Lending Institutions

Traditionally Building Societies were the prime source of finance for housing and property loan. Banks loaned money for more varied reasons but Building Societies were traditional lenders for house purchase. In more recent years the banks have become much more prominent in arranging home loans. There is a wide choice of mortgages now available through banks, building societies and insurance companies. In recent years mortgage advice centres have become prominent.

It is very important for a person considering a purchase to assess the exact financial commitment involved. One must decide what is the best deal in the particular circumstances. As already suggested, it is best to obtain advice from ones Solicitor and Accountant before reaching a decision. Mortgages take different forms such as fixed term rates, variable rates etc. An indepth discussion of these is not realistic in a book of this kind. However it is certainly advisable to approach the lending institution at a very early stage. You will then see how much they are willing to lend you in principle. You will then know at what level who can enter the market. Lending institutions will require you to fill out an application form and to give them certain documentation including proof of income.

When a borrower and a lender enter into a mortgage transaction the lender takes a legal charge over the property. This is the security for the loan in the event that the borrower fails to repay the mortgage repayments.

The borrower's Solicitor will advise about the contents of the mortgage document before it is signed. It will be explained that if the borrower defaults in repayments the lender can apply to Court for an Order of Possession of the property. This however is usually a last resort and the lending institution will endeavour to come to a mutually satisfactory arrangement where arrears have arisen.

If a borrower gets into financial difficulty the sooner the lending institution is approached and the matter discussed, the better. The law is usually reasonable in allowing the borrower a period to pay off the arrears. The Courts adopt an overall approach in these matters but must at the same time safeguard that the lending institution's legal rights will be protected. If a lending institution gets an Order for Repossession of a property under a Court Order it has an obligation to sell the property at the best price and to account to the borrower for any excess realised on the sale. Therefore after the mortgage is paid off if there is a surplus then this balance must be refunded to the borrower.

Auctioneers

Although most property is bought and sold privately, property can also be sold by way of auction. Approaching an auction can be a daunting task for the proposed purchaser. In this situation the proposed purchaser's Solicitor will be instructed and will make the necessary preauction enquiries and will attend the auction itself. It will be essential before the auction to have the property surveyed.

The title will have to be investigated. The financial arrangements will also have to be put in place. On the fall of the hammer at auction you are committed to the purchase if your bid had been successful. This will involve paying a deposit immediately and paying the balance within a month.

Surveyors

Whether buying a secondhand house or a new house the proposed purchaser will be strongly advised to have the property surveyed. Looks can be deceiving and the outward appearance of a house can hide a number of hidden faults. A lending institution will insist in all cases in having property surveyed. The primary purpose of such a survey is to establish whether, if the borrower defaults, the property will make enough to pay off the mortgage. Although the surveyor's fees are paid by the borrower the primary purpose of the survey is to protect the lending institution's interests. It is therefore very much in the purchaser's interest to have his own survey carried out. A survey can be carried out usually at a reasonable rate and it is money well spent before proceeding with the decision to buy.

Fees and Time Scale

It is advisable when you first visit your Solicitor to get an estimate of the legal costs involved. Usually this will involve the legal costs of the purchase and the mortgage. The fee paid to the Solicitor will only be a part of the legal costs in a purchase and a major part of the legal costs will often be the other items including Stamp Duty, Registration fees, search fees and VAT paid on the Solicitor's fee. As will be appreciated reading this chapter the conveyancing process is a slow and tedious one. At the same time it is important that a specified closing date is agreed so that it is clearly understood when the transaction will be completed.

Stamp Duty

The following are the rates of Stamp Duty on property. There is no Stamp Duty on transfers between spouses.

0-	5,000	exempt
5,001-	10,000	1%
10,001-	15,000	2%
15,001-	25,000	3%
25,001-	50,000	4%
50,001-	60,000	5%
Exceeding	60,000	6%

A purchase of house valued at £80,000.00 will therefore carry Stamp Duty of £4,800.00.

Stamp Duty on mortgages does not apply up to £20,000.00. In excess to this figure 1% to the total amount is imposed.

Stamp Duty for Farmers

Government policy on farming is reflected in the Stamp Duty laws. Transfers or conveyances of family farms to sons or daughers are levied at half the rate outlined above. So for example a farm transfer or conveyance from father to son which is valued at £200,000.00 would be at the rate of 3% instead of the usual 6%. If a milk quota is attached to the land Stamp Duty would be extra.

"Young, Trained Farmers" attract a further reduced rate when buying or leasing. "Young" for the sake of definition means under thirty five years of age. "Trained" means having attended an approved farming or other third level course. A 'farmer" is defined as anyone whose total assets include at least 80% agricultural assets. These include land, forestry, livestock, bloodstock or machinery. Stamp Duty can be reduced to one third the normal rate. The Revenue Commissioners produce some very useful leaflets on this.

Registration Fees

The average Land Registry fee for registering a title is £250.00 while the Registry of Deeds fee is £52.00 normally which would be comprised of £26.00 on the purchase Deed and £26.00 on the mortgage.

Search Fees

Search fees can vary from £50.00 to £100.00 depending on the title and the extent of the enquiries to be made.

Planning Permission

Any house built since the 1st October, 1964 requires Planning Permission. The purchaser's Solicitor will ensure that the necessary planning documents are in order. An Architect's certificate will usually be required confirming that a second hand house was built in accordance with the conditions of the planning permission. Where a new house is being bought the planning documentation will also have to be in order. Similarly, if the seller has carried out works on the property which require planning the necessary documentation covering these works will have to be produced.

Easements

Land and buildings can involve other people's rights to or over the property, e.g. rights-of-way. All of these matters will be properly investigated also before proceeding with the purchase. Such rights can include rights-of-way, gaming rights, sporting rights or restrictive covenants. Enquiries in this regard will be made as part of The Requisitions on Title mentioned earlier.

Boundaries

Problems sometimes occur with boundaries and it is a matter for the purchaser to establish what precisely is being bought. The purchaser will be advised to check the boundaries and to retain a professional to ensure that these are clearly defined.

Searches

The purchaser's Solicitor will carry out certain searches prior to closing the sale including a search on the title known as Land Registry search or Registry of Deeds search, a Judgment search against the seller, a Bankruptcy search and Sheriffs and Revenue searches if applicable. These searches are carried out to ensure that there are no matters arising which could effect the purchaser's clear title.

Insurance

It is essential that adequate insurance is put in place covering the structure of the property when the purchase is completed. It is the seller's responsibility to have the property insured up to the date of the closing and then once the deal is completed it is a matter for the purchaser to insure the property.

The lending institution will also insist that mortgage protection insurance be taken out. This ensures that if the borrower dies that the proceeds of the mortgage protection insurance pays off the mortgage.

Selling Property

As will be seen from the foregoing the procedures on buying and selling are intertwined. The seller will have to give instructions to his Solicitor regarding the details of the transaction.

However, there are some differences involved in the selling and buying procedure. Many people who are selling will retain an Estate Agent to act for them in the sale of the property. You will need to give accurate information to the Estate Agent regarding the property. It is the seller's responsibility to pay the Estate Agent's fees once the transaction has been concluded. Discussions will take place between the seller and his Estate Agent as to the best way to sell the property, i.e. whether by private treaty or by auction.

The seller when instructing his Solicitor will have to provide proper information together with title to the property. In most cases the Deeds will be lodged in a bank or building society where the seller has obtained a mortgage. The Solicitor will take up the Deeds on the instruction and authority of the seller. It will be necessary to give the Solicitor details of the transaction or alternatively the auctioneer will give details of the agreement. Apart form the auctioneer's fees the seller's Solicitor fee will be payable together with VAT and any petty outlay. The major items such as Stamp Duty, Registration fees, Search fees etc. which will be payable by a purchaser will not be payable when selling. It will be the seller's responsibility also to give all the necessary details to the Solicitor to enable the him or her to reply to the Requisitions on Title.

Family Home Protection Act, 1976

This Act prevents the owner of a family home selling it without the prior consent of his or her spouse. Section 2 of the Act defines the family home as a "dwelling in which a married couple ordinarily reside". It is the responsibility of the seller's Solicitor to draft the correct Family Home Protection Act Declaration which will be handed over to the purchaser's Solicitor on completion. The seller will also have to give specific instructions regarding what fixtures and fittings are included in the sale. It is in the interest of both the seller and the purchaser to agree on all items of potential future dispute at the beginning to avoid disputes arising near completion or after the sale has closed.

It is the seller's responsibility to hand over "vacant possession" of the property on the agreed closing date. The seller should ensure that the keys of the property are not handed over to the purchaser until completion has taken place and until advised by the Solicitor that all matters are in order and that the balance of the purchase monies have been paid. As already mentioned if the purchaser fails to compete on time the seller will have certain remedies which will include charging of interest on late payment. The seller may also be entitled to forfeit the buyers deposit if the buyer fails to complete the transaction. There may also be other grounds for an action for breach of contract by either party depending on the terms agreed.

Conclusion

It is hoped that this chapter gives the reader an idea of what is involved in the purchase and sale of property. It is an onerous and painstaking task and can be a stressful time for the purchaser or seller, however, this stress can be greatly eased by the helpful advice and professional way in which the Solicitor for purchaser or seller carried out the work involved.

4 SUCCESSION LAW

Introduction

Where a deceased person dies without having made (executed) a valid will that person is said to have died "Intestate".

However where a deceased person dies having made a valid will that person is said to have died "Testate" and the will in due course shall be admitted to Probate. The term "Probate" derives from the Latin phrase "Probatum" which means "To Prove". So the will must be proved in common Form of Law. The law regulating wills is as complex as it is varied. Historically it dates back to pre Roman times. In modern times and more particularly since The Wills Act of 1837 Freedom of Succession was in use.

The 1837 Act allowed a Testator (Male) Testatrix (Female) to dispose of his/her Estate both real and personal as one so chose. This meant that a person who had executed (made) a valid will could leave his/her property to anyone he/she wished. It is a perception which still exists with some people today.

In the 1960's however a golden age of legislative reform occurred in Ireland. On the 22nd December 1965 the Dáil introduced Legislation which by virtue of Section 1 of the said Act states "This Act may be cited as The Succession Act 1965". The Minister for Justice appointed the 1st January 1967 as the date upon which the Act came into operation. The effect of the Act was to repeal and consolidate old Statute Law. This piece of law moved away from the idea of freedom of succession. Instead it was designed to reflect the family values expressed in the Constitution. It conferred a legal right to a share in the proceeds of a will between married people. It also gave the children of a deceased person a right to claim a piece of their dead parents' estate. (Estate does not mean a large country manor or indeed a type of road transport, it simply means land, money, goods, valuables or buildings which can be sold and given a value). The children's right to claim is based on the failure of the deceased's moral duty. To balance this shift, the Succession Act retains many of the other freedoms which were formally part of the older law. This older law, taken from the Wills Act of 1837 still survives in Northern Ireland today.

What Does a Will Look Like?

Once a will has been registered and proved in the Probate Office the result is a Grant of Probate of issues. The Grant of Probate is a sealed High Court document which establishes that the will has been formally validly executed. Once the Grant of Probate issues the will becomes a public document and any member of the public has the right at this stage to inspect the said will.

The Central Probate Office is located in the Four Courts Dublin. In addition to the Probate Office in Dublin there are 14 District Probate registries located throughout the Country they are all attached to the Local Circuit Court Office. For example, the

District Probate Registry in Sligo is located in the Court House in Sligo and covers both the Counties of Sligo and Leitrim.

Here is a simple will of an imaginary retired man who owns his own home, has personal assets and lives on his pension.

I, Joseph Black, Company Director, of Rocklawn, Rochestown, Co Dublin, make this my last will and testament, hereby revoking all former wills and testamentary dispositions heretofore made by me.

1. *I appoint John White and Michael Grey as executors of this, my will.*
2. *After payment of all my Lawful Debts and Funeral Expenses I give devise and bequeath all my Estate both Real and Personal whatsoever and wheresoever situate to my wife Ann Black unto and for her own use absolutely.*
3. *In the event of my said wife Ann Black predeceasing me, I give devise and bequeath all my Estate, both Real and Personal whatsoever and wheresoever situate to my three children Joe, Jack and Jane equally.*
4. *The residue of my estate I give to the Saint Vincent de Paul Society in Ireland. In witness whereof I have hereunto signed my hand this 1st day of March, 1996 One Thousand Nine Hundred and Ninety Six.*

Signed:
Joseph Black.

Signed by the testator as and for his last Will and Testament in the presence of us who in his presence at his request and in the presence of each other all being present at the same time having hereunto subscribed our names as witnesses.

Michael Green
Solicitor
Dublin

Patrick Orange
Legal Assistant
Dublin

In the above example which is a little unusual but not unacceptable a number of things occur.

Firstly the reader will be drawn to the legal terminology used and probably ask is it necessary?

What if the Signature is not Witnessed?

The will must be signed by the Testator (Male)/Testatrix (Female) after the date and before the attestation clause (i.e. the clause above the witnesses signatures. They in turn must sign their names in the presence of the Testator/Testatrix. They do not witness the will but merely witness the signature.

The Signature

It's advisable that the signature of the Testator/Testatrix appears at the foot or end of the will after the date and before the attestation clause and witnesses signatures.

It might surprise most people to know that the testator need not sign his own name or that his name need not be in his own handwriting - a signature by some person in the testator's presence and by the testator's direction will be acceptable as the alternative to the signature by the testator himself. The person so signing on the testator's behalf may sign in his/her own name or in that of the testator.

Any of the following methods have been used and approved by the courts: The testator's initials; an assumed name; a former name; signature using a rubber stamp; a seal or a descriptive phrase.

A testator may attempt to sign his will but be physically incapable of doing so. Therefore the courts will uphold any mark that is made by a person and witnessed as such.

The rules on signatures are many and varied. These few rules are just some of the formalities required when signing a will. They are meant to indicate to the reader the enormous complexity and danger of not having a will properly drawn up.

The Gifts Under the Will

In our sample will, the reader will notice our imaginary testator left all his goods to his wife. Had the Testator not done so then by virtue of the Succession Act 1965 the spouse has a legal right share to one third of the total Estate after deductions for debts where there are children, and where there are no children she has a legal right share to half the total Estate after deductions for debts. Where there are no children, she is entitled to half the estate.

She may choose another route in this scenario. Where there is a gift under the will, for example the family home or something more valuable, is left under the will to a third party, she may elect to take that instead of her legal right share of one third or one half, whichever the case may be.

Living together - not married

A cohabitee is a person who lives as man or wife but is not married to the other partner. In this case such a person is not entitled to a legal right share. If such a person is not catered for under the terms of a will, they will get nothing.

Separation or Divorce

The testator, i.e. the deceased person can, before death, block the legal right share to the spouse. Should the couple separate the testator may be able to obtain his wife's agreement to disinherit herself from her legal right share. This can be done by registering a separation agreement.

An alternative would occur in separation or divorce proceedings where the court could make an order extinguishing this legal right share. A spouse would therefore get nothing.

The Residue or Remaining Portion of the Estate

After the will has been granted probate by the probate office, the estate having been distributed by the executor with the guidance of the solicitor, the residue is now given to charity. As already mentioned any gift that would fail under the will for whatever reason would not render the will invalid but would go to the residue. It is always prudent to allow a residue in a will even if there may not he one foreseen by the testator.

Executors:

An Executor (Male)/Executrix (Female) are the person(s) appointed by the Testator to administer his Estate. The Succession Act also sets out the various powers an Executor has in relation to the administration of the Estate. Before this the beneficiaries cannot demand distribution. But creditors can still sue for their debts.

Ultimately in law what is happening is that the executor is passing the property on to the persons mentioned in the will in a caretaker capacity. Any gift of land or buildings must be transferred in writing. The will gives this effect.

Choice of Executor

Choosing an executor is best given some thought before deciding who that person will be. It is wisest to choose someone with business ability. The person should be honest to the community at large. It is advisable to name two Executors in a will. At times it is prudent to choose someone from outside the family as occasionally a family feud might emerge over the gifts as they are distributed by the testator. This person or persons would then be a neutral in any dispute. Where an Executor has commenced to administer the Estate and fails to complete the administration there are procedures whereby the Beneficiaries can compel the Executor to do so. This would involve a Court action. The solicitor of course would guide the executor's actions and ensure they performed the task correctly.

Failure of a Will

A will may fail for any number of reasons and the deceased will be deemed to have died intestate. Therefore his Estate will be administered by his Next-of-kin (if any). In the unlikely event of their being no Next-of-kin the State is the ultimate Intestate successor, and the Estate will be administered by the nominee of the State normally the Chief State Solicitor who is based in Dublin Castle. This will be done according to the rules of intestacy. It may suit some family members, when they have been omitted from the will altogether, for the will to fail and the rules of intestacy to apply. (We will look at these later in more detail). For now an explanation of a challenge by a child of the testator is in order.

Failure of Moral Duty by Testator

S (117) of the Succession Act provides the following: Where the Court is of the opinion that the Testator had failed in his Moral Duty to make proper provision for the child within his means, it can order that such provision can be made out of the deceased's estate.

There is a high degree of proof required to show that a testator failed in his positive moral duty to any child of his. It would depend on several factors including that child's position and prospects in life, whether the Testator has already in his Lifetime made proper provision for the child, the character of such an individual, the position under the will with regard to other children. All of these and other factors will be taken into account at the time of a court hearing to determine a failure of moral duty. If, for example, the claimant had received a private or university education from the testator during his lifetime this would weigh heavily against a claim but might not be fatal to it.

Intestacy

Where no will exists or where a will only covers part of a deceased's estate then the rules of intestacy apply. Where the deceased left no will his Next-of-kin becomes administrator of the Estate (Note: administrator for Intestate situation and Executor for Testate). The State will be the administrator as ultimate Intestate successor only where the deceased has no next-of-kin. There is a fixed method of applying the rules and they run on family lines. This could refer to immediate family such as a spouse or children or parents, or to more extended family such as uncles, aunts, nieces and nephews. It has often been known to grant an asset from an intestate person's relative. This would be like winning a mini lottery to the person concerned. Experts such as genealogists may at times be used to make the connection between an intestate person and a hopeful claimant. Alternatively, should a person feel they have a valid claim to property or from an intestate estate, they should contact a solicitor who can advise them accordingly.

Spouses and Children

If a spouse is left with no children upon the death of the intestate person, that spouse will take all the property. If, on the other hand a spouse has issue (the legal work for children), they would receive two thirds of the estate and the children one third. If there is issue and no spouse - then the issue share equally. Children of the deceased or issue of the deceased from a previous marriage or children of the deceased born outside wedlock would qualify as issue. The above would be subject to taxes and other deductions. If those children of the marriage or as otherwise mentioned are not alive their place can be in turn taken by their children equally.

Other Beneficiaries

After spouses and children, other close family members would inherit an intestate estate. A deceased's parents would receive the benefit in the absence of these. If both parents were alive they would get equal shares. If on the other hand only one remained alive, that parent would get everything.

If all the above were dead, then brothers and sisters would get the estate equally divided between them. If any of these were dead, their children would divide that share equally and so on.

The Succession Act gives a system of counting the degrees of relationship. Again a solicitor would be in a position to assist a client in determining whether they have a valid claim to a share in an intestate's estate.

If there are no relatives whatsoever in existence the goods and property of an intestate would go to the State. The Minister for Finance however, as the person who holds the responsibility for ultimate intestacy in the State can surrender this right in favour of any individual. This could mean that, if a person who is no blood relative of the deceased intestate has possession of the assets, the Minister can let them have them, in whole or in part. It is the Attorney General who advises the Minister in this regard.

Altering a Will

Any alterations to a will after signing will be invalid. There is a presumption that an alteration is made after the execution. However if proof is furnished that the alterations were made before Execution (or signing) then this shall be acceptable. When an alteration is made it is strongly recommended that such alteration be initialled or signed by the Testator and witnesses and refer to the amendment in the Attestation Clause (the part where the Testator signs the Will). This proof could take the form of sworn statements by the witnesses or expert handwriting specialists giving evidence. It has happened that ultraviolet light and examination has been used in the past to discover what was written or scratched out.

Revoking a Will

This refers to cancelling an existing will, whether for good or with a view to changing its contents. A will is automatically revoked upon the marriage of the testator. The exception to this is if the will is made with a view to such a marriage. This would have to be mentioned in the will itself. It could take the form of an ordinary opening sentence, e.g. "I am getting married and I wish to make this will".

Another method of cancelling a will would be in writing. So in our sample will earlier the testator revoked all former wills. Alternatively an addition to the will - known as a codicil - duly signed and witnessed properly by two witnesses can revoke a former will. It is not enough to have only one witness. This would leave the first will as valid, even if this was not the intention of the testator.

Destruction burning or tearing of the old will is also a valid method of revoking a will. However it must be done by the testator or someone in his presence and by his direction with the intention of revoking it.

A photocopy of a will may be good and an application made to Court to have same proved in terms of the original where the original is lost - so it is crucial that a photocopy be maintained.

The above situations are by no means the end of the story. There are many other ways in which a will can be revoked or altered. The obvious and wisest course of action is to use a Solicitor to firstly draw up and word a will properly. They would in turn keep the original safe and secure. Wills are still lost in modern times. This loss can substantially alter a deceased person's estate and the division or otherwise of the assets. It would be advisable that the Testator or Testatrix would inform a trustworthy person of where the original Will is, e.g. the Solicitor's Office, Bank etc.

Taxation

Property passing under a will or on intestacy is liable to probate tax as well as other forms of taxation like gift tax. A person's solicitor would be able to outline these taxes in more detail. However for the purposes of a will, and the duty of the personal representatives or executors in particular, probate tax is, amongst other things, a main concern. Again, the solicitor handling the estate of the deceased person takes care of all of this.

Probate Tax

Since the 18th June 1993 the taxable value of Estates above a relevant threshold is subject to a 2% Tax. This is Probate Tax.

What Property is Liable to the Tax?

Where the deceased was domiciled in the State or living at a normal place of residence within the State all assets wherever situate passing under a will or intestacy are liable to Probate Tax with the exception of those exempted.

Where the person is not domiciled in the State his or her property situated here is liable.

What about Property which is not Passed Under the Will or an Intestacy?

These are exempt from probate tax. Some of these are joint property in joint ownership, which passes to the survivor gifts made in the lifetime of the deceased. The proceeds of insurance policies which pass directly to beneficiaries. Pension entitlements which pass to dependents.

Exempt Assets

a)   Where the estate is valued for tax at less then £10,000. This limit is index linked.

b)   The dwelling house. This must have been occupied by the deceased as his principal place of residence. It includes contents and 1 acre of ground.

  i) Where there is a surviving spouse, then the Dwelling House is completely exempt from Probate Tax irrespective of the share (if any) passing to the spouse in that Dwelling.

  ii) Where there is no surviving spouse that portion of the Dwelling House passing to a dependent child or dependent relative is exempt. The dependent child/relative must

  (1) have normally resided in the house at the date of death and

  (2) had income not exceeding a specified amount in the year to the 5th April prior to the date of death (currently £4,149.00). A dependent child is defined as a child under the age of 18 years of age or if is over 18 years is in full time education. A dependent relative is defined as a relative of the deceased or of the spouse of the deceased who is incapacitated by old age or infirmity from maintaining himself/herself.

c)   Property passed to a registered charity.

d)   Heritage property

e)   Superannuation benefits arising on the death of the deceased and passing under the will or intestacy are exempt.

f)   Quick Succession.

If one spouse dies probate tax will be paid. If the other spouse dies within five years exemption extends to that part of his/her estate which has already been taxed, if a dependent child is left. If the surviving spouse dies within one year the dependent child requirement does not apply.

g)   Certain securities are exempt where the deceased was domiciled outside the State.

Who is Responsible to Pay Probate Tax?

The personal representatives are the primary persons responsible to pay probate tax. This is because they are legally responsible as a trustees of the estate. Should these not be available the beneficiary or person receiving the property has secondary liability. Probate Tax can be shown as an expense against Inheritance Tax on the beneficiaries gift. Probate tax is spread proportionately between more than one beneficiary in this case. It is worthy of note that where the probate tax is not paid within 9 months after death interest will accrue at the rate at 1.25% per month or part of a month. This interest cannot exceed the amount of tax. Certain cases of hardship could receive special treatment an application to the Revenue Commissioners. Again a Solicitor could give expert advice and assistance on such matters.

Procedures for Obtaining Grant of Probate or Grant of Administration

There are specific procedures in order to take out a Grant of Probate or Administration. A number of documents will need to be sent to the Probate Office, Four Courts, Dublin or to the District Probate Registry situate at the nearest Circuit Court Office. The assets and liabilities of the Estate must be established. Valuations of property owned by the Deceased or of balances of Bank accounts or other accounts must be established. A return to the Revenue Commissioners must be made setting out the assets and liabilities together with the probate tax return if probate tax is payable. A number of forms including the original Will and the Revenue Commissioner's Certificate of the assets and liabilities must then be sent into the Probate Office.

Where there is no Will then a Grant of Administration will need to be applied for. It will have to be decided in whose name the application for a Grant of Administration should be made. There are additional documents to be filled as the procedure is not quite the same as that which applies to an application for a Grant of Probate. When the Grant of Probate or Grant of Administration is obtained the Executor or Administrator must then release the assets and finalise the Estate in accordance with the Will or in accordance with the law which applies if there is no Will.

Conclusion

To the lay person the whole process of wills and probate may seem over complex, unnecessary and costly in time and money. To call it complex is a correct description. It certainly does take time and does cost money in tax and legal fees. But if a beneficiary receives a gift under a will or otherwise it is well worth the trouble to clarify the ownership of it rather than leave such issues open to challenge at some later date. Where a house or land is concerned it cannot be legally bought or sold until the title or ownership of it is clarified. At the end of the day, a properly executed and administered will makes the use and disposal of assets all the easier.

This chapter, if the reader considers it to be heavy and complex, does give an insight into the type of skill and training which is part of the everyday work of this area of the law.

5 EMPLOYMENT LAW

Regulation of the Employment Relationship

Employment never was a private affair. Most Western Governments see it as a public service.

The old view, and a view that still exists with some people today, was that of master and servant. In this outdated system the master, or the boss, had total power over the servant or the worker. However, the law, through court judgments and laws passed by various parliaments, have tipped this balance in order to create a more favourable working environ-ment in which that vital commodity, the worker, is properly protected. The attitude of the law is that the weaker party in the employment contract, i.e. the employee, must be protected by the intervention of the law. Thus the employment contract is almost unique as a private relationship which is subjected to a great deal of public regulation.

Compare the present state of Western economies with those of the 18th and 19th centuries where freedom of contract existed in the hiring and firing of staff. Large excesses of wealth were in the hands of a few. Poverty and disease were widespread among the masses. If the poor did not possess land or other property they had no rights. As the worker gained more rights through legal protection, simultaneously his standard of living improved to the level it is today. The worker is now seen as vital in the generation of wealth for the whole of society. However, the law did not turn completely against the employer but rather it gradually worked out what is socially reasonable. As will be seen the position of the employee has been strengthened but the employer, the boss, has not lost complete control. It is wrong to say that once someone is hired they cannot be fired. Once an employment relationship comes into existence, the law imposes certain duties and obligations on both parties which must be obeyed.

Employment Law is an area where there has been a huge amount of legislation introduced over the last twenty years. It is not possible in a book of this nature to deal with all the Legislative Acts passed over the last two decades. It is hoped however that the reader will get a good general introduction to the main aspects of Employment Law in this chapter.

The Employment Agreement

Every normal employment agreement is built upon a contract, whether written, verbal or implied by the conduct of the parties. In this contract it is usual for terms to be outlined between both parties, such as hours of attendance, duties of employee, rates of pay or other payment in kind etc. Like any commercial contract that is agreed - even verbally - the law presumes its existence. That means it is up to the person denying its existence to prove that it does not exist, and not vice versa as is commonly thought. What about the situation where an employment contract does not come into effect immediately, for example more than one year after it has been agreed? An ancient law which is still valid today requires that for such a contract to be enforceable it must be in writing.

Express Terms

Express Terms are terms that are spoken about and agreed between both sides. They are then put in writing or are discussed by the parties in establishing the details of the working relationship. In the past, only the larger or more conscientious employees tended to use a standard written contract. Now the Terms of Employment (Information) Act 1994 requires an employer to give to his new employees, or to his current employees if they so request, a written statement of the terms of employment, within 2 months of the commencement of the employment or of the request. This effectively forms an employment contract and must include the following details:

1. The full names of the Employer and Employee.
2. The address within the State of the registered office or place of work. If this does not exist a statement that the employee is permitted or required to work in various places.
3. The title of the job or nature of the work.
4. The date of commencement of the employment.
5. If the contract is for a fixed amount of time, the date at which it ends.
6. The rate of pay, method of calculation and frequency of payment, e.g. weekly, fortnightly, monthly etc.

7. Terms as to hours (including overtime) and whether it is a condition of employment that employee can avail of overtime.
8. Terms relating to paid leave (other than paid sick leave)
9. Any terms regarding
i) incapacity for work due to sickness or injury and paid sick leave and
ii) pensions or pensions schemes
10. The period of notice which the employer is required to give and entitled to receive (whether under law or under the terms of the employees contract of employment) to end the employee's contract of employment or where this cannot be given, the method for determining such periods of notice.
11. A reference to any union or association agreements which directly affect the terms of the worker's employment. The reference must name such unions or associations. This must be done even where the employer is not party to such agreements.
12. The Employer may give all the above information by making reasonable reference to them, e.g. where the employee might have reasonable access to them during the course of employment, then the employer could say for example "as held by the shop steward" or "posted on the company notice board".
13. The statement must be signed and dated on behalf of or by the employer.
14. The Employer must keep a copy of it for 1 year after the employee commences.
15. The relevant Minister can enforce these by court order.

Restraint of Trade Clauses

These are express terms which may be used by an employer to put certain restraints on the employees either during their employment or after they leave that employment. They could, for example, restrict the use of information or expertise built up by the employer, or provide that the employee does not work for a rival in the same area, or not start a similar business in direct competition to that employer.

There are some rules however on the formulation of these:

1. The restraint must not be so wide in terms of time, space and subject matter as to render it unreasonable.
2. There must be a reasonable justification for it.
3. The scope of the restraint must be proportionate to the rights which are sought to be protected.
4. The restraint cannot be excessive in time. 1-2 years would probably be acceptable.
5. The restraint cannot cover an arbitrary or random geographical area. The extent of an acceptable geographical area will depend on whether the employer's business is in a rural or an urban area.
6. The restraint cannot prevent a former employee from engaging in unrelated employment or business activities.

Implied Terms

These are terms which are not written into the contract, nor are they spoken about in the pre-contract negotiations but arise by law. They are equally as important as express terms but it can be more difficult to establish their existence in the event of a dispute. Such terms exist in every employment contract, but a term will only be implied either if it is necessary in a business sense to give efficiency to the contract or if it is automatically implied into the contract by the operation of the law.

Officious Bystander Test

This is a test most often used by the courts to imply a term into a contract. It arises where a term is so obvious that it need not be mentioned. The test therefore is, if the term were to be mentioned an officious bystander would immediately comment "oh, of course".

For example an employee in a gunpowder factory would be prohibited from smoking on the job or a person employed to proof read documents would be required to be able to read - regardless of the fact there might be nothing expressly mentioned in their contract to this effect.

The courts have developed various duties owed by the employer to their employees. The following are examples:

1. The duty of the employer to provide a reasonable working atmosphere. Where an employee is subjected to a working environment that is so bad that the employee cannot reasonably be expected to endure it and leaves, their resignation may constitute an unfair dismissal, known as constructive dismissal. It is very difficult to prove constructive dismissal and an employee should make every

effort to put up with the situation and only take the drastic step of leaving where they feel they have absolutely no other choice. One situation where this implied duty of the employer was breached was where a secretary was boycotted by management, given no work to do and isolated completely from her colleagues. She eventually left and successfully claimed unfair dismissal.

2. The duty of the employer to take reasonable care to protect the health and safety of their employees.

This places a responsibility on the employer to provide a safe work environment for their employees and specifically to provide safe staff, equipment, place and systems of work. The duty is not absolute but a high level of responsibility is placed on the employer and if an employee is injured in the course of his employment owing to the negligence of the employer, then the employee will be entitled to claim compensation. However that compensation may be reduced if it can be shown that the employee's injuries were due in part to the employee's own negligence, for example in not operating a piece of equipment in the way they were taught to do. There is also a corresponding duty on the part of the employee not to damage the property of the employer. In practice such damage will usually be grounds for disciplinary action against the employee, possibly leading to dismissal in extreme cases.

There are also implied duties which an employee owes to their employer. Examples of implied terms are:

Duty of Employer to provide a good working atmosphere

Breach of this implied term occurs where the working situation gets so bad that the employee is forced to leave. So in the case where the secretary was boycotted by management and given no work to do the company was held liable for breach of this implied term.

Implied Duty of Fidelity

This is a bit like the restraint of trade mentioned earlier. Here an employee is required to remain faithful to the employer. This operates in several ways and includes any breach of confidence by the employee where the business of the employer is of such a nature as to require secrecy. However unless the confidential information in question is expressly protected in the contract by a restraint of trade clause, this implied term will only protect what are known as 'Trade Secrets', an example being the secret recipe for Coca-Cola. Thus this term will only protect the most extreme of confidential information and an employer would be well advised to protect their confidential information, such as customer lists, by means of an express restraint of trade clause.

Implied Duty to Employer outside of working hours

As mentioned an employee may not abuse valuable secrets of his/her company after they leave. However simple commercial good will is still within this protected category and must be guarded by an employee outside working hours. For example working for a competitor or as a competitor (nixers fall into this category) without permission of the employer is an activity that could lead to dismissal. An employees general conduct outside work may be grounds for discipline or dismissal depending on that conduct and the nature of work. Criminal activity which would include assault, theft and more serious offences would be adequate grounds in many companies for dismissal of that employee.

It is unlikely that non criminal sexual behaviour outside the workplace could lead to dismissal but such activity has been known to lead to that conclusion.

Implied duty on employee to be of good behaviour in the workplace

The continuous and persistent pursuit of any activity which may damage the company's business may lead to dismissal.

For example the clerk who wore a badge stating "Lesbians Ignite" got the sack as he refused to remove it and frequently served the public on behalf of the company. The dismissal was justified as certain people might take offence to this and according to a tribunal, they in turn could take their business elsewhere.

There are also some duties which are mutual to both the employer and the employee, for example the mutual duty of trust and confidence

Duty of Mutual Trust and Confidence

This is probably the most important of all implied terms. There must exist this trust and confidence between both parties. When it is lost or denied by one party either by words or course of action the contact fails and the offended party may, in the case of an employer justifiably dismiss an employee, or in the case of an employee, may leave and pursue a course of constructive dismissal against the employer. We will discuss these later.

Another example is where an accountant performed overseas contract work for his employer. He was asked on short notice to go abroad on a particularly important assignment for the company. This time happened to coincide with his pre applied-for holidays and the birth of his first child. He refused and was dismissed. An employment tribunal or court found his dismissal was reasonable. This confidence and trust may be shattered where an employee is required to do a dishonest deed. A driver was ordered to tamper with the dockets on petrol receipts and record inaccurate amounts in favour of the company in which he worked. He refused and was dismissed. A tribunal held that his dismissal was unfair. He got damages against the employer for the wrongful loss of his job.

The implied term or duty on an employer not to injure and to take reasonable care of his employees.

This is better dealt with in another chapter in the book but it is necessary to say that should the employee be injured in the course of employment due to the omission or carelessness of his employer this would involve a breach of contract (as well as other legal grounds) by or on behalf of that employer and would result in damages or compensation being paid to the employee.

Note: However if an employee does some careless act where he or she injures a fellow employee, or a third party or does accidental damage to some item or thing then it is not anyway certain that the employer will indemnify or pay for such wrongful acts. In fact an employer is quite entitled to sue a careless employee for the damage they may have caused. Usually though an employer will not sue a careless employee in practice but may simply dismiss them.

This duty on the employee goes so far as to protect the employers property. So if an employers property is destroyed or stolen while in the care of the employee - that person could then be liable for the loss.

Other implied terms

The above is not by any means the complete list of implied terms from law. The Dáil has manufactured terms through legislation or Acts. It is important to note that the implied terms mentioned up to this point can be altered by agreement between employer and employee. Legislation on employment however cannot generally be altered by agreement. This is a good example of the protection which government extends to the labour force.

One big problem is for a worker to qualify under much of the employment legislation protection he or she must have a minimum of fifty two weeks continuous service done with that employer with not less than 8 hours worked in each week. This does not mean however that a worker cannot use law to remedy an otherwise wrongful dismissal. Here are some statutory implied terms.

Minimum Notice and
Terms of Employment

An employer wishing to terminate the contract of employment of a worker must give the following advance notice.

1.   If the worker has been in continuous service for less than two years, one week.
2.   If worker has completed more than 2 years continuous service but less than 5, two weeks.
3.   If worker has more than 5 years continuous service but less than 10, four weeks.
4.   If worker has more than 10 years continuous service but less than 15, six weeks
5.   If worker has more than 15 years service, eight weeks.
If an employer should default in paying this the sum can be recovered from him through a tribunal or rights commissioner to include holiday payments.
To qualify for this statutory notice a worker must have served for 13 weeks continuously.
An employee in turn must give one weeks notice if he or she has been in continuous employment for 13 weeks or more.
Either party can waive or abandon the notice entitlement either in the contract or later but the waiver must be clear and not open to different interpretations.

Employees' rights to receive written information regarding their employment is covered under the Terms of Employment (Information) Act, 1994. This provides that an employer is under a legal obligation to provide an employee with a written statement of the terms and conditions of employment. An employee to be entitled under this Act must work eight hours or more in a week and have been in continuous service of an employer for a minimum of one month.

The information which should be included in the written statement of the terms and conditions of employment. An employee to be entitled under this Act must work more than eight hours in a week and have been in a continuous of an employer for a minimum of one month. The information which should be written statement includes the full names of the employer and the employee, the address or registered office of the company, the place of work, the job title or description, the date of commencement of employment, the expected duration of the contract, the rate of pay, the method of calculation and frequency, e.g weekly, monthly etc., hours of work including overtime, entitlement to paid leave, occupational schemes, sick pay etc. Any dispute under this Act should be referred to a Rights Commissioner. The recommendation of the Rights Commissioner can within six weeks of being issued be appealed to the Employment Appeals Tribunal.

The foregoing notice periods are provided for under the Minimum Notice Act 1973. Disputes arising under this Act should be referred to the Employment Appeals Tribunal.

Holiday Pay for Employees

This is based on a minimum amount of paid holiday leave amounting to three weeks per annum or proportionally less where you have been employed for under one year, e.g twelve months = three weeks, six months = one and half weeks. Leave must be taken in the current year or in the six months of the next year. You are covered if you are over eighteen years of age and have worked for the same employer for at least 120 hours per month. If under 18 the requirement is 110 hours per month. Any dispute regarding annual leave can be dealt with by the employee, by a Trade Union, the Minister for Enterprise and Employment or by the Courts. The relevant Acts here are the Holiday (Employees) Acts, 1973 - 1991.

Part time workers are fully entitled to paid holiday leave. This is based on a minimum of 19 days for 1400 hours worked. The Minister can enforce these entitlements by prosecution of the offending employer. Normally however this is not necessary as holiday entitlements are catered for by the employment contract or by union agreement.

There are entitlements also to leave on public holidays of which there are eight: New Year's Day, St. Patrick's Day, Easter Monday, 1st Monday in June, 1st Monday in August, last Monday in October, Christmas Day and St. Stephen's Day.

Maternity and Work

Legislation provides basic rights to the female employee when pregnant

1.   The right to maternity leave
2.   The right to return to work at the end of the leave period. This right cannot be changed by agreement, but more leave than is provided for under law can be agreed.

The minimum requirement for maternity leave for the female worker is fourteen weeks paid leave provided you satisfy Social Insurance Contribution conditions plus an optional four weeks unpaid leave.

There are certain notification procedures and time limits. The employee must notify the employer in writing at least four weeks prior to the intended leave and provide a medical certificate confirming the pregnancy and the expected week of confinement. If an employee wishes to take an additional four week's unpaid maternity leave written notification must be given to the employer at least four weeks prior to the end of the paid maternity leave.

No notice of dismissal, suspension or redundancy can be given while an employee is on maternity leave. Any dismissal arising from an employee's pregnancy of matters connected with same will be regarded as an unfair dismissal and should be dealt with under the terms of the Unfair Dismissals Act 1977 - 1993. The foregoing maternity rights are provided for in the Maternity Protection Act 1994. This Act also provides for the father's leave entitlement where the death of the mother occurs within fourteen weeks of the birth.

Equality

In the mid 1970's due to EEC laws several important equality Acts came into being in Ireland. Their objective was equality of pay between male and female workers. They established equality officers and the Employment Equality Agency to decide on this. An enquiry can be made to these through the Department of Equality and Law Reform Tel 01 6605966. The laws in this area only apply to those persons who are employees. Persons such as sub-contractors are not employees and cannot avail of the legislation.

How it operates

In order to use the system in existence a grieved employee must first identify a fellow employee of the opposite sex. This person is called the comparator. This person must be engaged in "like work" for more pay and must work for the same employer. However this does not exclude employers albeit in different companies who have some corporate link for example a company with otherwise independent subsidiary companies would generally qualify. A disadvantage which is evident for the claimant can be the definition of 'like work'.

When the Equality Officer has identified a valid claim every effort is made to be reasonable in the approach to the offending employer. The employer might not even be aware that there is inequality in the workplace. However should an employer unreasonably resist the recommendations of the Equality Officer and Labour Court, the Courts may issue an order to that effect. Prison maybe the ultimate destination for anyone in breach of such.

An equal pay claim should be made in accordance with the provisions of the Anti-Discrimination (pay) Act, 1974. The employee should firstly make the claim to the employer. If the matter is unresolved then it may be brought to an Equality Officer. An Equality Officer's decision may be appealed to the Labour Court within 42 days. A claim to be valid under this Act must be made on a comparison between men and women working for the same employer and that they must also be working in the same place.

Gender as a requirement for a job

The law will not allow a method which uses certain other grounds for discriminating between male and female workers. An employer must be able justify to a high degree any discrimination. Physical strength could be grounds for excluding female employees but it would have to be justifiable. Similarly dexterity in assembly work may be justifiable grounds for hiring more female employees. It is wise practice for employers when choosing employees to use some form of test before selecting workers for certain jobs where too many of one or the other gender are accepted.

The Employment Equality Act, 1977 provides that it is illegal for an employer to discriminate on the grounds of sex or marital status. Selection for employment cannot be based upon such. No discrimination is allowed in respect of conditions of employment including working conditions, hours of work etc. It also deals with such matters as sexual harassment.

Sexual Harassment

First we must attempt to define this. The European Union Commission's definition is... "conduct of a sexual nature or other conduct based on sex affecting the dignity of people at work, including conduct of supervisors and colleagues".

Ultimately, if an employer fails to ensure that sexual harassment will not occur, he or she will be liable to pay the offended employee compensation. Freedom from sexual harassment has become an implied term of the contract of employment. Breach of this can result in an award against the offender in Court. It may also be actionable under different areas of civil law or maybe, depending on the severity and if physical contact is involved, a case for Gárda involvement.

A code of practice issued by the Dept of Equality and Law Reform to educate staff and employees includes:

1. Outlawing sexually suggestive pictures and calendars
2. Leering and offensive gestures.
3. It recommends to employers to advise female employees to avail of female supervisors in other companies if none exist in their own firm.
4. Outlawing of sexual suggestions and innuendoes.
5. Importantly, it states that each employee is entitled to decide what behaviour is acceptable in the workplace.

   Even though the recommendations are not law at the time of writing, any employer who follows them will have every chance of avoiding a court action against them should such behaviour occur in the workplace.

The Employment Equality Agency acts as a watchdog in the area of discrimination. It is made up of representatives of various interest groups including employers and women's' organisations, trade unions etc. The members are appointed by the Minister for Labour. It can commence legal action against organisations or persons who practice discrimination.

Dismissal

Generally either side can leave or terminate a contract of employment at will. (This is not the same for other types of contracts). Even if the person is in a "permanent job" he or she can be fired, unless the agreement says otherwise.

On what ground can an employer dismiss an employee? There are three main areas or grounds which justify a dismissal namely capability, competence and conduct. (the three C's.) The overriding factor on all of these is that they must be "reasonable". It is important for an employer to establish reasonableness before he or she dismisses an employee.

Capability

It mostly concerns allegations that the employee is physically unfit or sick and unable to work. The employer is obliged to prove this and to act fairly in doing so. Where a person is injured and wishes to return to work, an employer, should they wish to do so, must establish that the person is unfit to work, not vice versa. There is no duty on an employer to provided alternative work or light duties.

Competence

This is rarely used. It would be difficult for an employer to turn around after hiring a person for their skills and claim that person no longer has those skills.

Conduct (or more appropriately Misconduct)

This is the most used ground in which dismissals are held to be valid. Unlike the other 2 grounds this, if severe enough, could result in summary dismissal. Summary dismissal is 'the sack' without the use of fairness of procedure. It may well be immediate. A warning to employers though, is that if summary dismissal is unfair they may well be liable to pay compensation of the employee. Some examples of the type of misconduct, and which must go against the more serious and important terms of contract, are:

1. Wilful refusal of an order
2. A dangerous or risky activity which would place the employer in danger of being sued.
3. Fraud, embezzlement or theft.
4. Physical violence against a member of staff or another person.
5. Any other occasion where the written or agreed terms of the contract of employment say so.

Unfair Dismissals Act 1977 and 1993

These important pieces of legislation provides much of the employee protection used today. However if an employee does not qualify (remember a person must be employed for a minimum of eight hours per week continuously for at least fifty two weeks) he or she can still use other legal remedies.

An employee has up to six months to seek a remedy under the Acts or twelve months where exceptional circumstances exist. If an employee is successful under the Acts he or she will be entitled to a choice of remedies, one of which must be agreeable to the employer. These are:

1. **Re-engagement**

   This is a resumption of work under the same terms as prior to the unfair dismissal.

2. **Re-instatement**

   Here also a return to work but the terms may vary. This could include doing different work or some other change to things as they were before.

3. **Compensation**

   If neither of the other remedies are acceptable to both parties a sum can be paid in compensation. This can be a significant figure as the Act allows for up to 2 years salary to be paid. So for someone on £20,000 per annum a very nice lump sum could be awarded to them in a settlement.

Constructive Dismissal

This occurs where the work situation is so intolerable as a result of the attitude of the employer or fellow employees that the worker is forced to leave. This is equally as valid ground as straight dismissal for the purpose of the Acts. Some more examples of constructive dismissal would be: Racial or other insulting behaviour by boss of staff on an ongoing basis so as to form a pattern; breach of any of the implied terms mentioned varied, especially denial of confidence or trust etc. These categories do not end but can be broadly defined as a situation so intolerable that the worker accepts the breach of contract by the employer. Before this course of action is followed it is best to seek advice from a Solicitor.

What steps should an employer take to avoid problems with Acts and other legal consequences?

As soon as a person employs another it is important that certain procedures be laid down generally knows as grievance procedures. This not only gives an employer advance notice of problems in the workplace but gives the troubled employee a path or release valve. Most misunderstandings are solved at this stage. It is unfair of an employer to expect a worker to think of taking grievance steps when they are not formally introduced to them.

Stage 1

Where an employees performance or discipline falls below an acceptable standard the employer would move to implement the following.

a)   Hold a counselling session with the employee. Try to find out on a 'one-to-one' what the problem is about. The purpose of this is not to discipline the worker but rather try to understand their situation. A neutral approach should be used.

b)   If the matter does not resolve itself the following procedure may be adopted.

Stage 1 - Verbal Warning after the worker states his /her case
This should state -

The drop in standards

The required improvement

When the matter will be reviewed again.

   What the next steps will be if no improvement is made.

Copy of the verbal warning should be dated and recorded and put in the worker's file. Warnings are best issued in the presence of a fellow manager (if necessary from another company) and an employee's representative.

Stage 2
Written Warning
This takes the form of the verbal warning again with the worker being first allowed to state their case.
This warning should be signed for by the employee. A copy should be kept on file.

Stage 3
Final Written Warning / Suspension.
This should be issued by a senior manager. This should state, after the worker has stated his or her case:
The standard required of the worker.
The date at which the matter will be further reviewed.
The action that will be taken if the required improvement does not take place.
It must be clearly stated that dismissal will take place.

The warning should be signed for by the employee.
Copy of the warning must be held on file.

Stage 4
Dismissal
Where the employee fails to improve he or she will be dismissed. Beforehand however there must be adequate and appropriate investigation and consideration by the company. A meeting by the company with the employee and representative outlining the company's position to the employee; and full consideration by the company of the employee's position.

Proportional Penalty

Often the situation can arise where, due to the severity of misconduct, an employer can proceed to the final written warning stage. Where gross misconduct by the employee occurs, as mentioned earlier, summary dismissal is open to the employer. However it is not advisable for an employer to presume every breach of conduct is a sackable offence. It is equally valid to fine an employee providing adequate warning has been given. When assessing any misconduct, account must be taken of the employees nature, personality, history, family and other situations. Other penalties may be withdrawing of bonus entitlements after adequate warning.

Suspension

Suspension for an offence may be implemented after due consideration by the employer. There are two types, namely, suspension with and without pay; suspension with pay is the more advisable route for an employer. This may be used when an employee's conduct is being investigated. Again it is prudent to use fairness before a decision to suspend. Suspension without pay may be used where the evidence is such that the employee is very likely to be justifiably dismissed but is being investigated. Suspension without pay is tantamount to dismissal without formal notification.

If allegations against an employee could involve any legal action against them then it is in the interests of fairness that the worker be advised to take independent legal advice.

Making a Claim

An employee has six months to make a claim under the Equality or Unfair Dismissal laws. In exceptional circumstances this can be extended to twelve months. When a worker feels a claim is justifiable, he or she may contact the Department of Labour who will issue a claim form. This form will be sent by the Department of Labour to a Rights Commissioner or Equality Officer depending on the type of claim. It is always prudent to consult a Solicitor to formulate it. The Rights Commissioner or Equality Officer will examine the claim and issue recommendation. If this is not followed though by the employer it may be then appealed to the Employment Appeals Tribunal. The employer has a very short time to appeal a recommendation against them. It is therefore vital for this reason alone to consult immediately with a solicitor.

Failure of an employer to comply with a recommendation from an Equality Officer or Rights Commissioner will result in these being enforced by the Circuit Court. The ultimate result of a breach of a court order is prison or a heavy fine.

When a worker is not an 'employee'

It is common for confusion to prevail when an employee is considered a contractor. The advantage for the employer is that they do not have to pay employers' contributions to PRSI; avoid unions; avoid pension schemes; avoid PAYE returns and insurance but in many cases it provides the biggest advantage of all: it avoids labour laws as outlined above!

The Dáil and Courts have long been aware that this system was open to abuse and have moved to remedy it.

Whether an employee is a contractor or not has led to a lot of cases in Court (since self assessment in Taxation was introduced as an option for employees, the confusion became even greater – especially since the Revenue Commissioners call this taxation for the "self employed"! Generally any employee can remain an employee under the protection of labour law and still avail of self assessment. It does not fundamentally change the nature of the existing employment contract, unless they so alter the terms as to agree to become self employed contractors. The advantages to both sides are numerous in the short term).

By labelling workers as contractors in the past employers sought of avoid their obligations. However since 1993 the law has closed many of the loopholes. The protections extended since then are many and varied. Loopholes exist however, e.g. the use of fixed term contract (i.e. from the commencement of employment to a time fixed in the future, usually under one year). Where a person is employed under such a contract from a year to year basis there must be a break of at least three months between each recurring contract. Otherwise the person will be considered within the cover of the law.

Prior to a 1993 law a person supplied by an employment agency or other firm as a 'temp' had no comeback against an employer who was not paying their wages or employing them directly. Now that employer is responsible if they would otherwise have unfairly dismissed the employee.

An employer or employee who is doubtful as to their status in the employment relationship should consider professional advice. Whilst acknowledging the valuable contributions of unions and other associations like I.B.E.C. many people, for one reason or another, fall through the net. It is common for individuals to assume things exist in this most valuable of contracts that have no grounding in reality. The times to consult are before an offer or acceptance is entered into, any change that affects the work relationship of mutual trust and   confidence, and at the end of the work agreement whether this is by choice or otherwise.

How to tell: Employee or Contractor.

It has been seen that it is vital that a worker knows in advance what his or her status is. Several tests have been devised by the Courts to enable the distinction to be made.

1. The 'Control Test'

    This is a modern first choice by judges. The old way was to determine the master and servant relationship. Now it depends on who gives directions and who obeys. In other words who does a worker report to. This is a matter of degree and can vary. In the case of a highly skilled worker the amount of control would be small. This type of person may still be an employee but it shows that the control test is limited.

2. Taxation.

    If a person is on schedule D 'self employed' tax it is merely an indicator that they are a contractor. It is by far on its own not conclusive proof of such status.

3. The Integration Test.

Whether a worker is sufficiently integrated into the firm as to deny the fact that they are in independent contractor.

4. The Declaration Test.

    If a written contract exists and the terms declare and identify the relationship as that of a contractor, the law will not proceed any further in its examination.

5. Multifactorial Test.

    This looks at all the parts of the relationship, e.g. how is a worker paid; who controls them; the type of tax; entitlement to holiday or side pay; etc

6. The Organisation Test.

    Whether the worker is working for themselves or someone else. This could apply in certain franchise and similar situations like existing agreements on certain government outside services. The thing to notice here is whether the person assumes the risk of profit and loss.

7.   The Elephant Test.

This probably best describes what the Courts look for. It encompasses all the other tests and tries to look at the situation as a whole.

8.   The Justice of the situation.

This is something to be aware of in particular situations where there is a large burden of responsibility resting on the employee/contractor. If the employee/contractor is not in a position to carry such a burden the law may often look for those who can and construct the relationship in this manner. So for example if an employee/contractor injures a third party and does not have the means to compensate that person for their injuries a judge may take this into account when considering the offending person's employment status. It has happened that they were held to be an employee.

Redundancy

When an employer dismisses an employee by reason of redundancy the employee is entitled to a lump sum payment equal to:- a half week's remuneration for each year of continuous service when aged between sixteen and forty one years or a week's normal remuneration for each year of continuous service when aged between forty one and sixty six years and the equivalent of one week's normal remuneration. The upper limit is £13,000.00 per annum or £250.00 per week.

An employer who proposes to dismiss an employee by reason of redundancy must give the employee notice in writing of the proposed dismissal not less than two weeks before the date of dismissal. A copy must be sent to the Minister for Labour at his office in Dublin. An employer can be prosecuted for failure to comply with such provision. The employer must hand the employee a completed form RP1. The RP1 form must be given to an employee who has more than 104 weeks continuous service. The RP1 and RP2 forms provide a system where an employer can regain sixty percent of a redundancy payment given.

Redundancy Defined

An employee is dismissed by reason of redundancy if his dismissal comes within any of the following circumstances:- (a) his employer has ceased or intends to cease to carry on the business for the purpose for which the employee was employed (b) the requirements of that business for the employee to carry out work of a particular kind in the place where he was so employed have ceased (c) his employer has decided to carry on the business with fewer or no employees (d) his employer has decided that the work for which the employee had been employed should than be done in a different manner (e) his employer decided that the work which the employee had been employed to do should be done by a person who is capable of doing other work for which the employee is not qualified or trained. It is presumed that the employment is continuous and that the dismissal was by reason of redundancy unless proved otherwise. The relevant Acts providing for redundancy payments are the Redundancy Payments Acts 1967 to 1991.

Remember that in order to qualify for redundancy payments persons must have been continuously employed for 104 weeks between the ages of sixteen and sixty six years, they must be within that age group and he/she must be expected to work for eight hours or more per week for the same employer. An employee may not be entitled to redundancy if he is re-engaged by the same employer under a new contract for employment or re-engaged by a different employer on the termination of his previous employment.

Unions

Originally these were unlawful organisations. Around the turn of the century they were given permission by law to act as negotiators for their members. Without this legal permission the activities of unions would once again become unlawful and employers would be able to pursue court actions for conspiracy and trespass, amongst other things against their own workers during industrial disputes.

Most unions today are registered by the Registrar of Friendly Societies. They must also satisfy the Minister for Labour and lodge a deposit with the High Court.

If a union does not fulfil these criteria correctly they may fall outside their legal permission and the membership or officers may be personally liable to court action in an industrial dispute.

There has been a lot of legislation in this area but the law on trade disputes has been tidied up since 1990.

Strikes

Strikes: for a strike to occur a certain procedure must be followed by the union

1.   A union must be properly constituted.
2.   Use of a grievance procedure, if in place, must be fully observed.
3.   A secret ballot must be properly conducted by the union.
4.   Seven days strike notice must be served on the employer.
5.   Picketing must be fair. If it affects the business of a third party that person may take an action against the union.
6.   Placards must be accurate. To exaggerate or misinform the public could be actionable by the employer.
8.   The strikers may only communicate their grievance peacefully. They cannot intimidate or block the access of persons who wish to enter or leave the employer's premises. This would be actionable by the third party or the employer.
9.   The strikes must assemble at the picket site in proportionate numbers only.

Any person has a legal right of strike. First they must exhaust any remedies under a grievance procedure. Wildcat or unofficial strikes by non registered groups are generally unlawful and may lead to a legal action against the strikers.

The Industrial Relations Act, 1990 repealed the earlier Trade Disputes Act of 1906. It contains important provisions in relation to Trade Union activities. A Trade Dispute is defined in the Act as "any dispute between employers and workers which is connected with the employment or non-employment of any person".

Union policy over the last 10 years or so has been to cooperate with employers and government. In general they want of dispel the confrontational image and be seen as positive contributors. They do not wish to be associated with the 'lone-wolf' renegade who would abuse the mantle of their union membership in an attempt to intimidate the employer. Furthermore if an employer is properly and professionally advised they can head off any growing confrontation before it begins.

If the reader requires a more detailed knowledge of employment law or workers rights and obligations the reader should consult one of the many reference books on employment legislation or industrial relations procedures. If one is contemplating legal action under any of the employment legislation one would be well advised to consult a competent Solicitor in that area.

6 NEGLIGENCE AND PERSONAL INJURY

Personal Injury

Before outlining the structure of personal injury compensation it is useful to understand the idea behind it.

Every person has a right to bodily integrity which is guaranteed by the Constitution. It is only in very limited circumstances that the law allows one person to injure another, for example in self defence. Not alone are we not allowed to injure each other deliberately or intentionally, neither are we permitted to do so recklessly or negligently. For the sake of clarity, reckless means knowing there is a risk of injury to another and proceeding anyway. It could also mean not caring whether an injury occurs. Negligently means not knowing that a danger exists and allowing an injurious situation to persist.

The law of personal injury compensation draws on the Christian idea that we are our "brother's keeper". We cannot carelessly injure him or her. If we do we must account for our carelessness and attempt to reconcile with him or her for the injury. If we fail in this an injured party may apply to the courts for his or her just compensation.

Historical

In the 19th century the industrial revolution had a radical effect on society. Not alone did it take people from the farms to the cities but in the factories huge steam driven machines operated in an effort to maximise production. In this environment human misery was everywhere. Long hours in textile or steel mills often resulted in workers being injured or killed. They had very little right to compensation. Factory owners were so politically powerful as to be beyond the law, and the parliaments made the law so as to allow this sorry state of affairs to persist.

Fair-minded and liberal judges undertook the task of rectifying this most unfair of systems. They built upon very narrow areas of compensation law and through a step-by-step development provided that not alone should a victim be compensated for his or her loss but for their pain and suffering also. Secondly, and of equal importance, they sought to punish and make an example of the wrongdoers who had caused such terrible havoc to their fellow citizens.

Today the law demands that each of us operates to such a standard, that, should we fall below it and cause damage, we may be held accountable for that damage.

Put simply anyone who causes damage where a duty to take care exists (the "neighbour principle") and is in breach of that duty, will have to pay compensation.

How Compensation Claims Operate

Liability or blame for negligent acts can arise in any situation. But for an injured person or plaintiff to succeed he or she must prove the following:

a   The defendant owes the plaintiff a duty of care.
b   There is a breach of that duty which was reasonably foreseeable to the defendant.
c   That breach of duty caused the accident.
d   The plaintiff suffered injury.

Generally speaking points (a) and (b) maybe a foregone conclusion as they apply in most accidents, i.e. someone is usually to blame. Cause and damage can often be a little more difficult.

One further point is that it is no defence for a defendant to say that as far as he was concerned there was no risk of injury. The standard is what a "reasonable man" in the situation of the defendant would have thought or done.

Proof

Let's look a little closer at the four things a plaintiff must prove to succeed in an action against a defendant for personal injury.

The Duty of Care

The categories are well established and include: road users owe a duty to other road users; occupiers of premises owe a duty to other entrants of that premises; a duty exists in certain cases not to make false statements; a manufacturer owes a duty not to circulate dangerous products; builders owe a duty not to construct dangerously defective houses etc. There are many more categories. It depends on the circumstances as to when these arise. For example, an employer owes a duty of care not to negligently injure his employee. (Remember 'negligently' means that an offending person may not be aware of the source of danger). The categories are not closed.

The Breach of Duty

The standard of what a 'reasonable man' would do is compared to that of the person causing the injury. If the standard of such persons is below that of the reasonable man that person is in breach of his or her duty of care. A court will look at all the characteristics of the person who may have caused the accident. It will consider their conduct, their physical attributes and in particular their mental condition. So if a person is foolhardy by nature this will not protect him or her from the consequence of their actions. A court will also objectively consider a persons knowledge and their perception and memory. A defendant is therefore expected to know the basics of everyday life for example that fire burns, water drowns, dogs bite etc. Further to this, if a person holds himself or herself out as a knowledgeable or experienced person in any one field the burden will be increased on their standard of care.

In other words a person who may be fixed with blame for an injury should have considered the

a)   probability of an accident occurring.

b)   the size of the loss should it occur.

c)   the burden of taking precautions to avoid the harm (i.e. the cost)

Therefore if the burden is less than the probability multiplied by the loss caused that person would be held negligent. i.e.

Burden < Probability x Loss.

An example illustrates this. A mechanic worked in a garage, No eye protection was provided. The mechanic was blinded when a splinter of steel entered his eye. The company were held liable in negligence. The cost of providing eye protection was slight compared to the risk of injury, which was medium, by damage which was caused, which was great.

An example of how this can be used as an effective defence is the following. A signalman in a railway company had to climb a ladder in order to work on a train signal. He fell and was injured. No safety cage was provided. A court held that the cost of providing safety cages on all such ladders on a national basis was so large as to outweigh the risk of accident and the damage caused on this occasion and the company were found not to be negligent.

The Risk

The degree of risk varies. What constitutes unacceptable risk to one judge may not be unacceptable to another, using the standard of a reasonable man. The test to determine risk is the foreseeability test. This test can be described as the sort of risk a reasonable man would foresee were he in the place of the person causing the accident. Some examples will help to show this. A hostess at a church party requested two men to carry a large tea urn down a narrow hallway. One man lost his grip and six children were scalded. Was that hostess expected to reasonably foresee that such an accident would happen? The reader might say "probably not". However if one of the men carrying the urn was not physically strong or not of a responsible nature, then he could be held to be in breach of his duty of care as he should have reasonable foresight of an accident.

However, a reasonable person does not need to cater for all the risks which he/she may reasonably foresee. If this were so it would make life intolerable. The purpose to be served if sufficiently important can outweigh the immediate risks taken. A fireman on the way to an emergency was injured when the driver of the fire engine suddenly braked. A heavy jack, which was normally carried on a specially fitted lorry, was lifted onto the back of the fire engine as the lorry was out of service. When the fire-engine braked the jack shifted and injured his leg. The court held that saving life and limb justified the risk taken. Therefore even though an accident was reasonably foreseeable the situation excused it.

Cause

If a defendant by his or her action or omission of a duty permits the injury they will be held liable in causation. Another and more precise way of looking at this is "but for" the act or omission of duty, would the accident have occurred? In the next example a deceased person had taken poison. He had reported to a hospital because he was sick. He was sent home and told to contact his own doctor. After he died his widow sued the hospital and a court held that the hospital was in breach of its duty of care in not tending to the deceased. But the widow failed the causation test as she failed to prove on balance that 'but for' the hospital's negligence in not treating the deceased, he would have survived. Another source or cause may be the thing which causes injury while under the care or responsibility of the defendant, e.g. in cases of injury from noxious fumes, if they can be shown to "materially contribute" to the persons ill health, the defendant will be fixed with causation. Even where there is insufficient evidence to connect the source of the cause to the injury in the absence of any other medical explanation, the injury or damage will speak for itself and causation will be allowed.

A Break in the Cause and Effect

An interference with cause and damage will deflect part of the responsibility. An example will illustrate this. Heavy traffic in and out of a quarry had damaged the main road. Potholes were created which caused water to gather and freeze in wintertime. A motor cyclist skidded on this ice and while standing up was run over by a car. A court held that even though the driver of the car was liable the offending quarry which had reckless disregard for the dangerous state of the road had interfered with the cause and its effect. It therefore held the quarry to be jointly liable (or to provide a "contribution and indemnity") with the defendant driver. Here is a simple test for this. Should a second (or concurrent) wrongdoer be found liable in respect of the same damage, then he or she will be jointly accountable.

Foreseeability of Damage and Injury

A wrongdoer will be held to be liable for any damage which he can reasonably foresee, however unlikely it may be, unless it can be brushed aside as too far fetched.

In applying this rule the circumstances of each individual case must be taken into account. On the one hand justice demands that the wrongdoer should pay for the natural consequences of his/her actions and on the other he or she should only be held accountable for that which a reasonable man would foresee.

An example best explains this. If a driver crashes into another moving car it is reasonable to foresee that it will cause damage to that vehicle and injury to the occupants. If, however, the car which was struck careered out of control and crashed into a petrol station which in turn caught fire (even though it observed all of the fire safety regulations), causing an explosion which damaged nearby houses and resulted in loss of life, could a reasonable man be said to have foreseen this damage?

According to the law on remoteness of damage the answer is "yes". This would be the natural consequence of the careless driver's actions. Would a reasonable man be expected to foresee such a tragic situation arising? Most fair-minded people would say 'no' but the law recognises that should the merest possibility become an actuality it will be taken as foreseen by a reasonable man and the defendant will be liable.

This rule however in many of its circumstances is felt to be unjust. Even though it is the current test for foreseeability it sits uneasily in the minds of many legal scholars.

Certain factors may provide a cut-off point or cancel liability altogether. If a defendant can show to a court that he or she has taken all reasonable precautions they may avoid liability altogether. An example will show how this works. An automatic sliding door was alleged to have malfunctioned and struck a person on the face causing injury. As a defence the occupiers of the premises were able to show that the doors were in good working order. They conformed to an engineering standard recognisable by the court, they were properly installed by a competent firm, using qualified technicians and were regularly maintained. It was reasonably unforeseeable that they would cause injury. The plaintiff's case failed. The defendant had not been negligent.

Summary

At this point it might help the reader to understand more clearly what needs to be proven in order to undertake an action for compensation for personal injury.

Four things need to be proved in evidence.
1.   A Duty of care exists between the plaintiff and defendant. This is well defined within the boundaries of the "neighbours principle".
2.   A Breach of that duty has occurred. This involved reasonable foreseeability. "Reasonable" in this context does not refer to everyday expressions like "reasonably priced" or "let's be reasonable about this" but refers to an objective test of what a right thinking and practical person would say were they in the same position as the defendant.
3.   Causation must be proved to show that the defendant caused the accident by his or her acts or omissions of duty. This often involves engineers' reports or other technical evidence.
4.   Damage must be proved. This would normally be provided by medical reports from specialists in various medical fields.

These four factors are each weighed by the court based on evidence submitted to support each point. If on balance they are held to be proved, damages in the form of compensation will be ordered to be paid to the plaintiff.

Contributory Negligence

Contributory negligence arises where there is a lack of reasonable care by the plaintiff for his or her own safety. At one time the merest amount of fault on behalf of the injured person barred their right to any compensation for personal injury. Today, however, the law is not as harsh. Some of the blame if proved by the defendant may be apportioned (or divided up) between the plaintiff and defendant. An example will help to clarify this.

A person is negligently injured and is awarded compensation of £20,000. If, however due to that person's actions at the time, they were themselves careless and contributed to the situation which resulted in their own injury, the court might apportion 30% of the fault to them. Therefore 30% of the £20,000 being £6,000. The plaintiff's total award is £14,000.

The main point to be taken from this is that just because an injured person contributed through carelessness to their own injury, it is not always the case that it was "their own fault".

Surrender of Legal Rights To Claim

The law is very even handed when it comes to granting compensation. It does not remove the possibility of the parties themselves deciding whether fault should be waived before an event. Examples of this are everywhere and include signs in public places which attempt to get potential plaintiffs to surrender their legal rights. Such signs might include —

"The management of this establishment will not accept responsibility for any loss or damage whatsoever caused to vehicles or contents thereof while using this forecourt".

"Passengers carried at their own risk" etc.

These are examples of signs which may or may not have legal effect. It depends on the individual concerned. It also depends on the wording which will be read by a court in a very narrow way, on its positioning, and its visibility.

The most effective way of guarding against a compensation claim is to ask the potential claimant, in plain and simple terms, to agree to waive their rights before they enter into the action which might result in a claim. For example a neighbour lending a ladder to another might say: "Look John, as far as I know this ladder is perfect, but will you accept that in the event of it breaking I cannot be responsible for any injury or damage?" The neighbour will say "okay" thereby probably waiving his legal rights with respect to a potential claim.

Occupiers Liability

The recent revamping of the law in this area was a policy decision rather than any other. Recreational users of public and agricultural land presented a large amount of claims on these occupiers. The Occupiers Liability Act 1995 has clarified the position of the duty of occupiers towards visitors recreational users and trespassers.

Failure to Mitigate Loss

This refers to a failure on behalf of the plaintiff to minimise his or her injury after the accident. For example a person may be negligently cut. If that person does not attend a doctor and treat the wound, but rather allows the cut to become infected, that person will be held to have failed to mitigate the loss and would be entitled only to claim for the cut but not the value of the infection.

Seat Belts

Those travelling in cars and not wearing seat belts are normally fixed with contributory negligence of 15% - 25% of the total amount of their award. So, if a claim is valued at £100,000 it could result in a plaintiff only receiving £75,000 of an award.

There may be excusing circumstances for not wearing a seat belt. These include obesity, pregnancy, post operation convalescence, etc. However a person cannot excuse themselves from this duty just because they deliver goods. For example, a van-helper's argument that it was not practical to use a seat belt when the next stop was close-by was rejected by a court.

Prior Accidents and Time Limits

The normal time limit for an action in negligence to be brought is three years from the date of that accident. This is known as the limitation period. If time extends beyond this the action will become barred and then cannot proceed. This law is to prevent claims arising at the whim of a plaintiff.

However, in certain cases accidents which have occurred outside the expiry of the three year limitation period will be allowed to proceed. This depends on whether the person had prior knowledge of the injury or knew the identity of the defendant. The three year time limit starts to run from the time that such knowledge is received. An example will help to show this.

A person worked in an asbestos plant. No proper protective equipment was provided, but it was available on the market. Twenty years after leaving that employment the person is diagnosed as having cancer. That person, now possessing knowledge of their injury, has started the 'limitation clock'. They now have three years to issue proceedings against the factory (in the absence of any other explanation) from the date the condition is diagnosed.

Aggravated Injuries

A person may have at one time been injured. However the limitation period has now expired on that injury. If however that injury has been aggravated from a new source the limitation period will start to run from the time of aggravation. To take another example let's say a person was injured in an accident twenty years ago and had knowledge of the injury. If however that same injury is aggravated by a second accident the three year limitation period will again commence.

A Particular Weakness

If a plaintiff has a particular weakness and is injured it will be no defence for a defendant. A man with a proven disposition for cancer was working in a foundry. He received a splash of molten metal on his face which turned cancerous. The fact that he had this inherent weakness and was inclined to contract cancerous ailments was no defence. He succeeded in his claim for compensation.

Nervous Shock

A person can recover damages for personal injury not only to their physical selves but to their mental condition also. This can be the result of mental anguish causing medically "approved" damage. Post-traumatic stress syndrome is a recognised modern example.

This type of compensation has been identified by the courts for many years. Certain rules have been developed to restrain the type of nervous shock claims that can be made, the courts fearing that they would be otherwise swamped with cases of this nature.

An Explanation of Nervous Shock

A legal definition of a physical condition may not resemble the medical explanation for that ailment. The law is concerned with justice and is inclined to follow human wisdom gained from experience rather than medical science. Nervous shock, as an expression, is used by lawyers to describe a range of emotional disturbances which are clinically recognisable such as psychiatric or psychosomatic illnesses.

Types of Nervous Shock

There is no court action for mere mental suffering as there must be evidence of actual psychiatric damage resulting from severe grief or mental anguish. The law recognises an action for such injury by shock sustained through the medium of the eye or the ear, without any direct contact.

Outrageous conduct by a person may result in nervous shock and an action may then exist against the defendant. In the course of a perverted practical joke a man told a woman that her husband was critically injured in a nearby pub and that she was to go to him at once. The nervous shock suffered by her resulted in severe and permanent physical illness. The defendant was held liable to pay compensation.

An action would also exist where the person might expect an immediate physical injury to a relative or friend. Similarly injury or damage to an object close to the plaintiff may give rise to a cause of action.

The types of relationships between the injured party and the person to whom the injury occurred has been examined and defined by the courts. Even if the injury is apprehended and does not occur compensation may still be awarded. These include any relative, a spouse, a child, a friend, a fellow worker or even to a third party. Even where some horrific scene has been witnessed, though neither life nor limb has been threatened, that person could recover compensation. However, in the past, the courts stopped short of awarding compensation when the plaintiff, on seeing her pet cat killed in front of her eyes, suffered a nervous shock.

Nervous Shock: Epilogue

The legal damage known as nervous shock requires the support of a medically recognised condition to have it considered by the courts. Like all negligence actions it requires reasonable foreseeability on behalf of the defendants, to make it successful. The scope of nervous shock is closely linked to advances in medical science. The more recognisable medical conditions which emerge the more grounds which may exist for successful actions to be taken in the future. Ultimately it is a matter of public policy, which the courts often decide, whether the grounds for nervous shock will expand or gradually be reduced.

Damages

This is compensation in the form of money payable to an injured person by a defendant. A court will make an order to this effect when it finds for the plaintiff in an action. It is normal practice for costs to be awarded also. This means that not alone will a defendant have to pay his or her own legal fees and expenses but they will have to pay the opposite sides' fees and expenses also.

The term "damages" is different to 'damage' which is a reference to the loss or injury caused.

Not alone may an injured plaintiff bring an action in his or her own right but should the person die on the occasion of the injury or as a result of it, their next-of-kin could then pursue what is known as a "wrongful death action".

Types of Damages

Damages are awarded for <u>injuries</u> and <u>loss</u> arising because of them. The main types of damages to which the courts refer are:

a   Compensatory Damages

The idea of this is to put the plaintiff as near as possible to the position which they were prior to the injury as far as money can do.

b   Aggravated Damages

This is additional compensation for the injured feelings of the plaintiff and is awarded where the plaintiff has been treated in a manner which the court feels heightens the sense of wrong done to them.

c   Exemplary Damages

These are additional damages awarded to the plaintiff to teach the defendant that causing injury does not pay. Both aggravated and exemplary damages are awarded to punish the defendant.

Damages for personal injury are based on two types of loss, i.e. loss of earning capacity and other expenses, both since the accident and in the future and with regard to the plaintiffs pain and suffering, which also includes their loss of prospects in the future and the loss of those things which the plaintiff, but for the injury, enjoyed.

So for example take a person being injured at the age of twenty one. If that person were an active sports man or woman, and had a good training in a business or profession or any other type of occupation with some prospects the following would be considered in assessing damages by a court: Their loss of salary or wage since the accident and into the future if they were unable to return to work. (This is usually assessed by an actuary or accountant who specialises in statistics and life expectancy for the insurance industry). Their pain and suffering would be assessed by medical evidence taken at the hearing both since the accident and into the future; the plaintiff's loss of prospects in the future is assessed taking into account what type of person they are, what areas of work they are involved in and in general what the future holds for their careers.

The loss of enjoyment in our example might mean they had to give up the sport they enjoyed so much. This would be taken into account.

Finally loss of amenity are those things which a person can expect to enjoy in a civilised society for example a happy family and home life, relationships etc. If these are lost as a consequence of the injury they will be taken into account.

The judges, when they assess damages, take a matter of fact approach. The types of damages are calculated in accordance with the law and a sum is arrived at. To access the loss of future earnings well-tried formulae are used. There is no guessing. If a defendant disagrees with the size of damages awarded to his or her victim and feel they have grounds to do so, they have the option to appeal the size of the award, as distinct from the decision.

Conclusion

As the reader will see there is a lot of highly skilled and complex work in bringing an action in negligence through the courts system to a final successful conclusion. The plaintiff must not alone prove the injury but the cause of it also, taking reasonable foreseeability into account.

In order to succeed it is not simply a matter for the Plaintiff to prove that he or she was in an accident and that injury resulted. It must be proved on the balance of probabilities that the accident was caused by the negligence of the Defendant against whom the action is being brought.

A potential Plaintiff must first be advised properly as to whether such they has a good prospect of success if such claim is brought. There are many procedures to be followed in bringing such a claim to a successful conclusion. Where liability is in doubt a potential Plaintiff will have to consider whether it is wise to pursue a claim at all. In the event of a claim being lost the Court will generally (but not always) award the successful parties legal costs against the unsuccessful party. These costs can be quite significant.

From a practical point of view the defendant must be a person of some substance. There is no point in bringing an action, with all the expense and work involved if such a person has no means.

"Man of straw" is the old cliche used to describe such a person. Only in very limited circumstances is it worth the expense and effort. However many cases involve actions against persons who are insured.

Sometimes, when a plaintiff has what looks like a strong case, a defendant might make an offer to settle before a case is heard in court. This is often the request of the person's insurance company who would handle the claim, whether it arises because of a traffic accident or other injury. A defendant's Solicitor and Barrister would look for any form of contributory negligence to offset against the full amount claimed and use this as a bargaining tool to reduce it. Many cases are settled in this way but it would be foolish to think that one can bluff the opposition into settling. On the contrary. But an experienced litigation Solicitor, whether acting for a Plaintiff or a Defendant, would be in a position be to analyse not just the facts of the case and the law involved but the relative strength of each parties position.

A lot of initial preparation must be done before proceedings are brought in a personal injuries claim. Engineers reports, gárda reports and medical reports must be obtained. Full instructions must be obtained from the injured party concerning the facts surrounding the accident. The financial implications for the injured party must be looked at carefully in order to assess the "special damages". It is usual for a Barrister to be retained to advise on liability. Only where liability is admitted will it be then a matter of deciding exclusively on the issue of compensation. This is called "assessment only".

Most people know that it takes a certain length of time before a case comes up for hearing in Court. The delays are mainly due to the very large number of cases pending before the Courts an the fact that there are a limited number of Courts and Judges available to hear these cases. During the time awaiting trial there is an opportunity for both sides to negotiate a settlement and in fact the majority of personal injury cases are settled out of Court.

7 CONTRACTS AND AGREEMENTS

Introduction

Many people go through life totally unaware that contracts exist or that they make (or break) them almost every day.

Not alone do lay people do this but successful business men and women carry on in the commercial world completely unaware of the valuable asset the law has given them to secure their transactions. This chapter, therefore, is intended to give some understanding of what a legally enforceable agreement (i.e. a contract) is, what is required to form it and what the repercussions are in terms of compensation against those who breach it.

It is vitally important to realise that a verbal agreement is equally as enforceable as one which is written. The practical difficulty is that the terms of a verbal agreement may be more difficult to prove.

An Offer and an Acceptance

Every contract in order to be formed must have an offer from one party and an acceptance from the other. An offer is a clear statement of the grounds, or terms, on which that person is willing to contract. It can be in writing or verbal. Similarly it can be conveyed by a face to face encounter, by fax, by telephone or by e mail. The layperson should however be conscious of the fact that what may seem like an offer may be, what is called, "an invitation to treat".

"An Invitation to Treat"

This is a device often used in the commercial areas of trade or business. It invites people to tender an offer. For example, a multinational company might want an extension built on to their factory. They would then invite tenders from a panel of approved sub-contractors to provide a detailed breakdown of the price of different parts of the project. Usually the lowest total price is accepted.

Other, more everyday examples are auctions or advertisements. When an auctioneer during a sale strikes the hammer the bid (offer) is accepted. If an auctioneer sells "without reserve" he is obliged to knock down the goods to the highest bidder once he or she commences the sale.

In most cases an advertisement is considered to be an invitation to treat. A buyer replying to such an ad. is making an offer, and he cannot sue for breach of contract if the seller refuses to sell. However it has been held that a very specific advertisement, in which the advertiser undertook to do certain things if a consumer purchased their product, could be held to be an offer rather than a mere invitation to treat.

As mentioned in the chapter on buying property, contracts for the sale of land have special rules.

Acceptance

The definition of acceptance could be "the final and unequivocal expression of agreement to the terms of the offer". It is important to note that where there is more than one item or price on offer then to admit to "acceptance of your offer" will not be legally binding. For example an offer by tender to build a house was submitted to a prospective home owner. The builder who was offering submitted two prices. The home owner faxed back that he accepted the offer. The contract was never formed as the home owner did not indicate which price he was willing to accept. An offer can be accepted by actions also. To receive a ticket on a bus is an acceptance of an offer. The passenger offers the bus driver a fare which the bus driver accepts. A contract is formed. Similarly if a person receives an offer and without giving a reply begins to act under the terms of the offer, their actions would constitute an acceptance.

Counter Offers

A person can make a counter-offer instead of accepting the offer. This has the effect of rejecting the first offer. If the counter offer is in turn refused the initial offer cannot now be accepted.

With regard to counter-offers in particular and negotiations in general the reader should note that it is often very difficult for a court to tell the precise timing of such events. It can happen that during the course of negotiations over a period of many months these may become obscure.

Communicating Acceptance

As stated acceptance can be communicated by performing the act required rather than by a verbal or written communication. This is known as a unilateral contract. But an offer cannot have as a condition that should the offer not be replied to, the offer will be deemed to be accepted as an acceptance must be communicated whether verbally, in writing or by conduct.

For example in the recent past the practice of inertia selling, i.e. selling on approval was popular. This involved the posting of goods or samples to a person's home on the condition that "should we not hear from you to the contrary within twenty one days we will expect full payment".

In this case not alone is the receiver of the samples not obliged to pay but can charge the sender a fee for taking care of the goods while in their keeping. Furthermore the Sale of Goods and Supply Services Act 1980 makes such deliveries a free gift in certain cases.

Acceptance must be communicated to the person making the offer in order for a contract to be said to exist. When the person making the offer gets notice of the acceptance then a contract arises. This includes verbal, written, telephone etc.

An exception to this general rule is acceptance by post. This in known as the 'Postal Rule'. Once an acceptance is placed in a letter box at the post office even though the person making the offer is yet unaware of the fact of acceptance, it is deemed as "accepted" by the law. It is possible to avoid the implications of the postal rule by stating in the offer the manner in which the offer must be accepted.

International trading is an increasingly important aspect of offer and acceptance. For example the place of acceptance of an offer indicates the country in whose courts system a case may be brought should a breach of contract occur. Alternatively a contract may specify the country whose law is to govern the contract.

How an Offer is ended

An offer can be withdrawn or ceased. If this is done prior to an acceptance then no legally binding agreement exists. It is important to communicate the withdrawal or ceasing of the offer to the party on the other side, for should acceptance be clearly communicated prior to this a binding contract will arise, resulting in a possible court action for its breach.

An offer may be terminated in the following way.

a   Revocation

The person making the offer will need to show that the other party knew that the offer was revoked or withdrawn before they received the acceptance. Otherwise a binding contract or agreement could be held to exist. Again as in many aspects of offer and acceptance the terms of an offer can vary or nullify a rule. The postal rule does not apply to letters of revocation.

b   Rejection

Once a person has communicated their refusal to accept an offer they cannot then accept it.

c   Time Delay

The acceptance must be communicated within a reasonable time. 'Reasonable' depends on the context. For example an offer sent by e mail or fax from New Zealand would require an acceptance by a similar speedy method.

Most offers demand an immediate acceptance. The commodity being traded could have a bearing on this. For example perishable goods require an immediate reply whereas a land sale might be allowed more (but not excessive) time. The terms of acceptance may be dictated by the person making the offer.

d   Death

A contract debt may be fixed to a persons estate after their death, but a death may also frustrate a contractual obligation and remove its effect.

An Exchange of Promises

To form a binding agreement A promises to pay or give to B, on the condition that B promises to pay or give to A. There a contract in order to be formed, requires the intention as well as the action of both parties. If intention can be disproved, therefore, no legally binding agreement exists, and one cannot sue the other for its breach. However if a promise is contained in a deed under seal (this is a document drawn up by a Solicitor with a special seal fixed to it) then nothing needs to be given or promised in return. This deed takes effect on delivery. It need not, it appears be signed by the person making the promise. The reader should note that a gratuitous, or 'free' promise does not provide the basis for a contract when otherwise given.

Pre-conditions

This refers to a requirement to be fulfilled either before or sometimes after the main terms of a contract are fulfilled. Failure to fulfil a precondition (also known as a condition precedent) could result in an action for breach of contract.

Uneven Bargain

If the bargain between the parties is uneven the courts may strike it down and render it unenforceable. However generally the courts will not investigate the adequacy of the promise, goods or payment given in return, but will uphold the idea that a person is free to enter into a bargain. There are however many exceptions to this rule.

Past Favours

A person cannot enforce a contract when that which he or she has promised has already been performed prior to the present negotiations unless the past performance was intended to cover a future bargain.

Debts

There are two types of debts which people recognise. The first is a moral debt. This consists of a promise or understanding given by one person to another without receiving anything of value in return, for example a generous aunt giving a weekly allowance to her nephew. A moral debt is not, on its own, legally enforceable. A legal debt on the other hand is enforceable by the courts, and is grounded in a contractual agreement. If A does not pay the sum owed to B then B can sue.

Compromising a Debt

There are some well established rules in reducing debts or reclaiming debts - let us look at some of these:

At common law. If a sum of money is owed by A to B and B promises to take a lesser sum in full satisfaction, B, on receipt of this lesser sum, can immediately sue for the balance of the full amount. This is often called the rule in Pinnel's case and operates because A has not given B anything in return for the promise to take a lesser sum.

If however, a new element is introduced into the relationship for the compromise of the debt, the lesser sum agreement will be legally binding and B cannot then sue. Thus if B agrees to settle for a sum of less than the full amount and A gives him or her something (or does some favour) in return by agreement, B cannot then sue. If B however were to give the reduction to A in the form of a deed then the promise would be legally enforceable.

Collecting Debts

For one reason or another a debt becomes overdue. This occurs usually in the course of business and may drag on for a long time. It is therefore of some comfort to know that a solicitor may be able to recover the sum outstanding for his clients and get their own costs from the defaulting debtor. For the readers information the list below briefly outlines the legal debt collection process in the District Court.

a   A letter is sent by a solicitor to a debtor asking for payment within seven days.

b   If no payment is received a summons is sent by registered post to the debtor.

c   If the debtor wishes to defend his or her position they inform the court and the creditors solicitor. The issue is then decided by the District Judge.

d   If on the other hand the summons is ignored by the debtor, the creditor's solicitor sends a signed standard form known as a 'decree' to the district court office seeking an order or decree by default.

e   If this decree is ignored an "Instalment Order" is applied for and granted by the District Court. A copy of this is sent by registered post to the debtor.

f   If the instalment order is not complied with the Creditor may apply to the District Court for a Committal Order by issuing a Committal Summons. This is an application for the imprisonment of the debtor. The Creditor will have to give sworn evidence and the Court may make an Order for imprisonment or may make a Variation Order providing for weekly or other periodic payments by the debtor.

The bad news for the debtor is that on top of the sum owed they now owe the costs of all of this work to the creditor's Solicitor.

The logic of a debt situation is therefore clear. Should outstanding debts arise it is very important (unless a person has valid grounds to feel that a debt is not justified) to contact the Creditor at an early stage to try and renegotiate the payment. Should the debt be for a substantial sum, a Solicitor, as a professional negotiator, would perform this function

Other Types of Contract

Different types of contracts require different formalities. It is important to re emphasise that an agreement or contract can have equal legal effect if it is verbal. It does not always have to be in writing. The Terms of the contract, if in writing, help to clarify any disputes later.

Sale of Land and Buildings

Contracts for the sale of land, buildings need to be in writing to be legally enforceable. Again, these can be made up of different letters 'pieced' together to form a contract (outlining description, names of the parties and location, type of tenure or title and price) between both parties. The sale of interests in land need to be in writing. This topic has been dealt with in an earlier chapter.
A permission in land could be sale of things attached to land, for example fishing or shooting rights, the right to cut turf or timber. Where a permission only is involved there is no need for a written and signed agreement.

Contracts not to be performed within one year of entering the contract

To eliminate uncertainty surrounding the delay of such agreements the law requires them to be in writing and signed. Contracts of employment are covered by the same rule.

Specific Performance

Where legal requirements for a sale of land are not fulfilled and a Court is unsure of the opinion that an injustice exists it may give an order granting the wishes of an offended person.

Part performance could work against the person who maintains that there is no written contract and therefore no legal reason why they should be bound by their promise. An example will help to clarify this. If A promises B that once B moves into a house which is the subject of an agreement between them, A will than sign the contract of sale. Later, while B is living in the house A changes his or her mind and wishes to remove B. Note there is no written and signed agreement between them. B will be able to go to court and get an order forcing A to accept the contract of sale.

Hire Purchase Agreements and Loans

The law requires these types of agreements to be recorded in writing. If there is no written agreement they generally are not enforceable against the person who reneges, i.e. the borrower in most cases.

Consumer Contracts or Agreements

New EU Regulations now require that all contracts supplied to consumers and contain lists of terms (usually on the back, i.e. the small print;) must now be in 'easy to understand' everyday language. The new rules outlaw the use of legalese or nineteenth century language which until recently gave the suppliers an advantage over the consumer in the sense that the consumer often agreed to terms and conditions which they may not have understood fully.

A 'consumer' has a broad definition. Not only are they the person in the main street who purchases everyday goods but could also include companies engaged in trade or business, or others.

The European Communities (Unfair Terms in Consumer Contracts) Regulations 1995 apply to all standard contracts. Under the Regulations if the obligations of the business person results in an unfavourable situation for the consumer then a term shall be considered as being unfair. Where there is no doubt as to a particular term in the contract the meaning most favourable to the consumer will apply. The Director of Consumer Affairs is charged with the responsibility of enforcing this legislation. He may apply to the Courts to prohibit the use of unfair terms under these regulations.

Terms of an Agreement

A contract is composed of 'terms' and 'conditions'. It is useful to have an idea of the difference between them, and the possible fall out should they be broken or breached.

Terms are divided into two types these are.

1   Express Terms

These are agreed between the parties in discussions before final acceptance. They are different from implied terms in that they are written or spoken. An example of express terms could be delivery times available etc. Should they be breached they could lead to an award of damages against the offending party.

2   Implied Terms

These are implied or imposed onto an agreement by custom statute, common law, the constitution or the Laws of the European Union. Breach of a term entitles the offended person to sue for damages only.

These are necessary to the operation of the contract.

The breach of condition entitles the offended person to call off the agreement. They will not be penalised for doing so. It also gave them an opportunity to sue for damages.

Exemption Clauses

This is a term that is inserted into an agreement, again it may be written or verbal, which might exclude the seller or purchaser from an action or some responsibility.

An exclusion or exemption clause, in order to be effective must be capable of standing up to examination. A court therefore will scrutinise these. Therefore an exclusion clause inserted in the sale of a vehicle which read:- "maximum load 1200 kgs", failed to operate when a large number of people used the vehicle at the same time resulting in one being injured. "Maximum load" was held to refer to goods, not people, and as an expression in this case was self defeating. It is important then to have these drawn up by a lawyer where the consequences would be drastic should they fail.

Under the Sale of Goods and Supply of Services Act 1980, any attempt to 'contract out of' an agreement by inserting an exemption clause will be invalid unless such a clause is fair and reasonable. Similarly any attempt to 'contract out of' the legal responsibility as to description, merchantability (i.e. fitness for use), and fitness for purpose will be null and void. So for example if someone buys a pair of shoes which fall apart after 2 weeks of normal wear (remember one has a right to complain and be refunded up to 3 months after the contract has been made), it will not help the seller to say "I accept no responsibility for these shoes after I sell them".

Misleading Advertising

The government may now prosecute for any advertising which is misleading. Advertising in this instance is defined as the making of a representation in any form in connection with trade business craft or profession and includes immovable property. Misleading advertising can be defined as "advertising, which in any way including its presentation, deceives or is likely to deceive". The remedy for the consumer could be damages for breach of a duty serving from statute.

The Duty of Disclosure

In certain types of agreements there is a duty to disclose material or important information which has a bearing on the agreement. Therefore when a person discusses an insurance agreement with a company, that person is obliged to disclose all material facts when asked. Failure to tell could result in a policy not operating when it is required.

Unenforceable Contracts

Not every agreement is enforceable under law, Let us examine some unenforceable contracts and some reasons behind why they are so.

Illegal Contracts

Contracts to commit a crime or a civil wrong are unenforceable in the courts.

This is a matter of public policy. Policy or politics shape the law as we know it so it would not be sensible to allow anything which is contrary to public policy.

Some examples of these could be the hiring of a gun to commit robbery; an agreement to defraud the Revenue Commissioners (which is a crime in itself). Similarly private contracts or agreements to undertake litigation in the courts would be unenforceable.

Contracts to corrupt justice are void and unenforceable. For example a plaintiff was a victim of an indecent assault. She was given a cheque for £50 in return for a promise not to prosecute the defendant. She could not later claim damages for non payment of the cheque.

The encouragement of immoral acts or practices is contrary to policy. What is immoral is as much a matter of social standards as it is of law. However some examples help to give an idea. Any contract that promotes sexual intercourse outside the confines of marriage is illegal and cannot be enforced in the courts. This may be more frequent than one thinks, as agreements between couples who are not married to each other and who may have purchased property together could cause difficulties and legal advice should be sought in such circumstances.

Contracts which breach foreign law are illegal. For example when a person in Natal posted Irish Sweepstake Tickets to Dublin the tickets were never entered into the draw. The contract was illegal according to the law of the place where it was formed. In this case lotteries were illegal in Natal.

Statute can make contracts illegal and thereby unenforceable. Thus as we have mentioned in other chapters the Family Home Protection Act 1976 which will not allow any dealing in the family home without the free and written consent of both spouses.

Contracts for gaming or wagering are void unless conducted under licence. Therefore one cannot sue for unpaid I.O.U.s gained during a poker game.

Compensation for Breach of Contract

Damages or compensation is awarded to a victim of a breach. Their purpose is to put that person in the position (as far as money can do) that they should have been in had the contract been successfully completed. Unlike damages, or compensation, for personal injury, awards against a contractual wrong doer are not designed to punish them.

In assessing damages a court will look at grievance of the wronged person and add up the different types of loss in money terms until it arrives at a final figure.

Damages are measured or quantified, under different heard of loss. It is important to remember that when quantifying loss in contract other types of loss may also be assessed as a breach of contract is also a civil wrong which attracts different types of damages.

Measuring Compensation for Breach

These are generally felt to be of three main types

1   Loss of Expectation
     An example will best explain this. If John makes a binding agreement with Mary to sell her engine parts with a value of £1000. Mary knows the value of these parts during the rally season in Kerry in the coming year will make £2000, i.e. a rising market. John reneges on the contract i.e. a breach. Mary is then entitled to her loss of expectation. Mary can go and buy these parts on the open market and sue John for the difference between the original purchase price and the price of the expectation. (We are assuming that Mary was committed to reselling the engine parts on at £2000.).

2   Reliance Loss
     In our example (above) Mary may have hired a lorry or suffered some freight charge as part of the bad bargain with John. This would be a valid 'head of loss' which Mary may recover. Where the 'loss of expectation' is difficult or

impossible to asses a court may often rely on this sum to quantify the loss incurred.

3   Restitution

If Mary had paid John the £1000 prior to delivering a court would also add this loss to 1 or 2 above.

Punishing the Breach

Sometimes the above types of losses might not be clear or may be so small as to be of no consequence to the offended person. The courts could find that in this case that the conduct of the wrongdoer is so annoying that it will award damages to punish them. An example could occur where the breaker of a contract has calculated out the amount that he or she would loose where they to be sued for a breach. With this figure in mind they were able to sell on the goods for yet a larger sum of money, even taking into account a court award for breach against them. This could result in an unjust enrichment by the wrongdoer and an injury to be suffered by the plaintiff or person bring the action in court.

Other Losses

Like damages for personal injuries, damages for breach of contract involves to an extent the natural consequences of the breach, i.e. the 'knock on' effect.

An example here will help. The plaintiff owned a mill. A shaft in the works broke and had to be sent for repair. The transport company and the defendants (who repaired shafts) were so slow that they returned the repaired shaft late. The mill could not operate without the shaft. They sued the defendant for loss of profits.

If it can be shown by the plaintiff in this case that his losses were unforeseeable he would be allowed recover sums which would be lost as the result of the lateness of the transport company. e.g. loss of market resale price of flour if on the other hand such losses were the in "reasonable contemplation" of the mill owner i.e. if he should have foreseen this his damages or compensation should be reduced.

One could ask "why did he not have a spare mill shaft ready in the event of the main one breaking down?"

Failure to mitigate loss will also, if found by a court, go against the sum of compensation awarded to the plaintiff. Mitigate means taking steps to reduce the loss which flows from the breach.

The above rule is general only. There are several exceptions depending on a whole range of factors involved in the context.

Action for Agreed Sum

Where an agreement is made for a fixed amount for work done or goods supplied and is then immediately breached by the person who is paying, the offended party may then sue for the amount promised on completion. The other types of measurements of damages mentioned above will not arise e.g. those arising from the natural consequences of the breach, i.e. the 'knock on effect'.

Quantum Meruit:- as much as he deserves

This is a claim for reasonable payment. It can operate in several ways for example when a piece of the agreed contract is performed and is then not completed for some reason. Another common reason is where an agreement is so altered as to make it unrecognisable from what was originally said and agreed. An example of this type of fundamental alteration could occur where a where a building agreement got so distorted as to make it unrecognisable from the original prices submitted on the architects plan.

Damages are assessed by expert evidence (usually) and could involve quantity surveyors or other technical experts.

Other Remedies

A court could make an order that a contract be carried out to the letter. This is a discretionary power of the court and will compel the defendant to perform his or her part of the bargain. This remedy is subject to certain limitations.

Time Delay

The passage of time may extinguish the right to bring proceedings. Where a simple contract (such as discussed in this chapter) is involved the time limit is six years after the breach. Personal injuries which arise from a breach of contract incur a time limit of three years.

Mental Stress

The courts will allow damages in breach of contract for mental stress in certain limited areas. For example where the contract is for a holiday, recreation or entertainment, damages may be got for disappointment, vexation and mental distress.

Conclusion

We all make contracts. Sometimes they are serious, most times minor. The law as it developed in the 19th century ran purely on economic lines. This is why contract law gives mainly economic remedies and assesses damages on mostly economic grounds. Through its development contract law has developed many different types of rules. Although mainly founded on common or judge made law, equity has intervened to refine and make less harsh some of the sharper ends of the common law system. The purpose of this chapter therefore is to give the reader a flavour of some of the more prominent aspects of contract. Like any chapter in a small book like this it cannot cover every aspect. The reader is advised that should they confront a serious breach of contract a legal opinion from a Solicitor is the best course.

8 ROAD TRAFFIC LAW

Introduction

There are over one million cars in Ireland. As a result the law has been heavily involved in the regulation of these. The policy behind road traffic law is obvious. It is for the law to say who can drive, how they drive and what they drive.

Buying a Car

The seller of a vehicle has a lot of responsibility in law. The private seller however differs in the responsibility to the motor trader. The licensed motor trader has different obligations.

1.   When selling an altered vehicle he or she commits an offence if they sell it without a certificate to state that is has been altered. Alternatively they could apply to the Minister for the Environment for an approval certificate.

2.   The Sale of Goods and Supply of Services Act 1980 also applies to the sale of cars by anyone, either trader or private seller. This is a law brought in to protect the consumer.

Under this Act the consumer or buyers' rights, are covered as to ownership, sale by description, quality of the vehicle and guarantee. The law imposes a statutory minimum guarantee on the sale of all goods as to major defects which arise on a product purchased within three months of the time of that purchase. Notice it is a minimum guarantee of three months. Most motor traders give a one year warranty on second-hand or three years warranty on new cars. The terms of these may vary, i.e. different traders would cover different things but the law itself says that a purchaser can legally apply for a refund for a vehicle with fundamental defects within three months. A fundamental defect is anything which would render the vehicle unable to perform the duties it is meant to. This statutory guarantee applies equally to second hand cars.

A warranty or a guarantee from the garage, is on the other hand, a private agreement between the parties. It applies as to the terms laid out in it and is as legally enforceable.

Financing the purchase of a car.

Most vehicles purchased are financed by borrowing. The seller who, in agreement with a finance company provides a vehicle to a buyer is jointly responsible for the following:

a)   Any breach of contract for sale. So if a motor trader sells a defective car the H.P. company would be jointly liable. If the seller is bankrupt the H.P. company is caught for the refund or repair.

b)   Any misrepresentation of the goods. If the motor trader says the car has only 10,000 miles as shown on the clock and it has more both that seller and HP company are jointly liable as above.

Driving Licences / Motor Insurance

Most people know that a licence is required to drive a road vehicle. It is an offence for a person to allow another to drive their motor vehicle in a public place without a current driving licence or without valid insurance. Both the owner of the car and the driver can be held liable to these regulatory, but nonetheless criminal, offences. The driver or owner must show that he or she has the licence and/or insurance to disprove the presumption that they were not breaking the law.

Some people do not need a licence to drive on the road. These are

a   a member of the Gardaí driving in the course of their duty

b   People doing a driving test for obvious reasons, but they must hold a Provisional Licence

c   Members of the defence forces, driving State owned or controlled mechanically propelled vehicles during a period of duty or emergency.

d   Pedestrian controlled vehicles.

Obviously disqualified persons are forbidden from applying for a licence. It is an offence for such a person to apply.

Certificates of Fitness

A certificate of fitness is required to be sent with the licence application for people suffering from a medical or mental disability. People with drug disability or alcoholism or regular drug users must also supply this. The same approach must be used by any applicant who is 70 years of age at the date of the application. This certificate has to be produced annually. Three things are possible on receipt of an application for a certificate of fitness.

a) It can be refused. However an appeal to a District Court might reverse this. The District Court judge's decision is final.

b) The decision to accept or reject the certificate by the licensing authority could be deferred. This could cause problems for some applicants so the process allows for the deferral to be appealed also.

c) The certificate may be granted. It may also be limited to a specific class of vehicle e.g confined to cars only.

Either (b) or (c) may be appealed to a District Court also.

Speed Limits

If a person breaks these he or she is guilty of an offence. However, to gain a successful prosecution a Gárda must produce evidence of speed. The Road Traffic Act of 1961 lays out what a Gárda or other person can produce in court as evidence of speeding.

Evidence of Speed

The "uncorroborated" evidence of a Gárda cannot be used to convict a speeding motorist. This means that without some device with which to measure the speed of a vehicle a Gárda or that person cannot give a statement in court which on its own would result in a conviction of the accused.

On the other hand a device which would "corroborate" excessive speed could include an ordinary speedometer of a car, if shown that the speedometer was in proper working order. If a Gárda follows a speeding car at a fixed distance and measures that speed, this would be acceptable in Court and a conviction would result.

Naturally, from this the reader can therefore understand that a radar-gun is pretty conclusive evidence of speeding. Modern equipment is very sophisticated and allows little margin for error. However even radar can be interfered with by electric equipment nearby or the reading may be affected by other traffic on the road. Speedometer readings also allow for margin of error. As it is generally a mechanical device a margin of two m.p.h. would be allowed. Therefore where a person were to exceed the speed limit by two m.p.h. it would, in the absence of other evidence to support a prosecution, be unsafe to convict and the Gárda case would fail.

Other devices which have been used to pursue successful prosecutions were:

A stop watch test by two Gardaí over a measured distance of road. Ordinance survey maps were tendered in evidence as to the accuracy of the measurements.

Gárda motor cyclists and especially squad cars have specially fitted equipment to monitor the speed of vehicles computerised in-board video cameras record the pursued vehicle and give readouts of date, time and speed. It has happened in the past that two Gárdai's variation in their evidence to a court caused a sufficient doubt to allow a charge of speeding to fail. With state-of-the-art equipment Gardaí have an instant recall facility available to them.

On-the-spot fines for speeding.

The Minister for the Environment brings in the laws affecting traffic. In order to curtail the speeding on our roads which has reached epidemic proportions and to increase detection efficiency on-the-spot fines would greatly add to the system in place. At the moment every speeding prosecution must come before a Judge of the District Court. This requirement occurs because speeding is a crime. The presumption of innocence extends to the offending motorist. To try and convict a person on-the-spot and then impose a sentence in the form of a fine would seem to fly in the face of Irish legal thinking.

In many European countries on-the-spot fines are common. Whole sections of traffic are pulled over and each motorist is fined for speeding. Fines in excess of £100 are normal. If a motorist will not pay their car may be impounded there and then. Even if a motorist cannot pay immediately they will not be allowed to drive away until cast iron assurances are received by the police of their intention to pay the fine. This could involve hours of phone calls or maybe the raising of a bond or guarantee to pay the fine which is owed. All major credit cards are acceptable.

Other Main Driving Offences

The law views the use of a vehicle in a public place as a grave responsibility. Other crimes involving road traffic helps to underline this view.

Manslaughter

This is the unlawful slaying of another person. It is not murder, abortion or infanticide. This gives the classical definition of dangerous driving causing death. It was an indictable offence and was to be tried by a judge and jury. It requires a very high degree of negligence to be proved in order to gain a conviction. The ordinary standard of negligence is enough to provide compensation for injury, but this is not enough to prove manslaughter. That standards would approach recklessness.

A person may also be guilty as an accessory. This has occurred where the owner of a car, knowing the brakes were defective, told his workman to drive it on the road. The driver failed to stop as a result and killed a pedestrian.

Penalties for manslaughter may be a prison sentence for a term not exceeding five years penal servitude and/or a fine not exceeding £3,000 together with a possible disqualification or endorsement.

Dangerous Driving

The best way to describe this is to outline the section of the Road Traffic Act 1961 which deals with it.

A person shall not drive a vehicle in a public place in a manner (including speed) which having regard to all the circumstances of the case (including the condition of the vehicle, the nature, condition and use of the place and the amount of traffic which then actually is or might reasonably be expected then to be therein) is dangerous to the public.

This can be summarised by the words "driving in a manner" which includes speeding; driving while sleepy or drowsy; being involved in a collision; momentary lapse of concentration or going on the wrong side of the road.

Defences in court which are recorded as successful are actions because of some medical condition, for example epilepsy; receiving a blow on the road while driving; unconsciousness; an attack by a swarm of bees or a sudden mechanical defect. All these defences have this in common i.e that some force, other than their own free will, overcame their normal competence.

Where the prosecution failed to prove a charge of careless driving the Defendant may be convicted of a lesser charge of careless driving or driving without due care and attention.

In assessing whether any person is guilty of dangerous driving the Court will look at a number of factors. These include the speed at which the person was driving. The Court will look at all relevant circumstances and including the nature of the place where the alleged offence occurred, the amount of traffic in the area or expected to be in the area,whether pedestrians are expected to be in the area,whether it was a built up area and whether in all the circumstances there was a risk or danger to the public at large.

The penalty for dangerous driving and conviction is a fine not exceeding £1,000.00 and/or a term of imprisonment not exceeding six months

Drunken Driving

Introduction
There are four separate drunken driving offences
1.   It is an offence for a person to drive or attempt to drive a mechanically propelled vehicle in a public place while he or she is under the influence of an intoxicant to such an extent as to be incapable of having proper control of the vehicle, or
2.   to drive or attempt to do so in a public place while he or she has in their body an amount of alcohol which, after three hours of driving or attempting to drive, gives a concentration of 100 milligrams of alcohol per 100 millilitres of blood, or
3.   to drive or attempt to do so in a public place and has in his or her urine a concentration of alcohol in excess of 135 milligrams per 100 millilitres of urine, or
4.   to drive or attempt to do so in a public place where a concentration of alcohol on his or her breath exceeds a concentration of 44 micrograms of alcohol per 100 millilitres of breath.

A person cannot be convicted of all four separate offences but only one arising out of the same incident. A person can however, if charged under one offence be found guilty of another.

To gain a conviction under any of the above offences the prosecution must show evidence that

1. The defendant drove or attempted to drive
2. It must be a mechanically propelled vehicle
3. The occasion must be in a public place
4. The defendant was under the influence to such an extent as to have been unable to have proper control of the vehicle. This charge is often used where a defendant has failed to provide a blood or urine sample. This also covers drugs or a combination of both drugs and alcohol.

Proof

A Gárda can give evidence based on his observations that the defendant was unable to have proper control of the vehicle. If a doctor is called his or her observations may greatly aid the Gárda testimony. A Gárda merely stating that a defendant smelled of alcohol, spoke with a slurred voice and staggered, may not be enough to get a conviction. Failure to do other simple tasks like walk a straight line would help a Gárda case.

A Gárda need not inform an accused person of the precise nature of the tests, provided the person is properly cautioned and gives consent to a medical examination.

Consent must be given voluntarily. If not, the evidence of the blood sample will be excluded resulting in the collapse of the prosecution. Other similar standards are imposed on the Gardaí by the courts, failure of which may or will result in the exclusion of evidence by the prosecution. Some of these are

1. Breach of defendants constitutional rights
2. Unlawful interference with bodily integrity
3. Interference with the defendant's health
4. Lack of fairness on the part of the Gardaí
5. Blatant abuse by the Gardaí
6. Failure to properly caution at time of arrest or failure to caution at all.

There are many other legal devices whereby a case may be caused to fail. This is why it is vital to have a solicitor to defend a person so accused. There is an old saying:- "The person that defends himself in Court has a fool for a client". Nowhere else is this more true than in a drunken driving charge.

80 Milligrams in Blood

In an attempt to tighten the drunk driving law in Ireland the government introduced a proposal of 80 milligrams per 100 millilitres of blood.

Driving or Attempting to Drive

Driving can be proved by the evidence of a witness or witnesses. Often a person, when asked by a Gárda admits to the offence. See the chapter on crime where an admission to a person in authority is equal to a confession. This may be allowed as evidence against a defendant providing such a person has been properly cautioned. An attempt to drive is decided on what seems to the Court be the immediate intention of the defendant on the occasion in question.

"A mechanically propelled vehicle"

This is rarely a problem for the Gardaí to prove. It is usual for a Gárda to give the registration of the vehicle in question in court. A prosecuting Gárda may however have difficulty when arriving at the scene of a traffic accident, a vehicle is so badly disabled as to fail the description of "mechanically propelled". Similarly where a vehicle is so disabled due to breakdown or removal of the engine for example, it is no longer capable of being mechanically propelled.

The "A Public Place" Requirement

The prosecution must prove this. By definition it includes any public road, any street or other place to which the public have access with their vehicles. These descriptions however have wide meanings and could be summarised by describing them as any place where the public may be put in danger by drunken driving.

"Drunk in Charge"

This is difficult to define as it is so variable. However the following provide some guidelines.

1. If a person is owner of, or has recently driven a vehicle, he or she will be presumed to be in charge, unless they prove otherwise.

2. If a person is sitting in a vehicle, or is otherwise involved in it a Court must decide whether he or she has assumed

charge of it. The intention of the defendant at this point is crucial, or if a person has taken the keys and moves towards the vehicle, or if a person has the correct key to the vehicle. The distance of that person from the vehicle is relevant.

Penalties

A sliding scale of penalties now exists along with a fine and an endorsement. For repeat and serious offenders a prison sentence not exceeding six months may also be given. Here is the sliding scale of disqualification, from the Road Traffic Act 1995.

Reference Number	Concentration of alcohol	First offence under section concerned	Second or any subsequent offence under same section
(1)	(2)	(3)	(4)
1.	(a)Not exceeding 100 millgrams of alcohol per 100 millilitres of blood: (b)Not exceeding 135 millgrams of alcohol per 100 millilitres of urine: (c)Not exceeding 44 micrograms of alcohol per100 millilitres of breath	3 months	6 months
2.	(a)Exceeding 100 milligrams but not exceeding 150 milligrams of alcohol per 100 millilitre of blood; (b)Exceeding 100 milligrams but not exceeding 150 milligrams of alcohol per 100 millilitres of urine; (c)Exceeding 44 micrograms but not exceeding 66 micrograms of alcohol per 100 millilitres of breath.	1 year	2 years
3.	(a)Exceeding 150 milligrams of alcohol per 100 millilitres o blood; (b)Exceeding 200 milligrams of alcohol per 100 millilitres of urine; (c)Exceeding 66 micrograms of alcohol per 100 millilitres of breath.	2 years	4 years

The general power of the Gardaí to stop and search was, with a few exceptions, limited until recent times. "Road blocks" for example were limited to the checking of the mechanical condition of road vehicles. Gardaí however consistently stretched these powers in the exigency of their duty. The notion of a Gárda with a flashlight coming out from behind a wall or a ditch at night is well known to motorists. Whilst Gárda powers were traditionally held in check by the courts a new departure (possibly as a result of the perceived upsurge in crime) has taken place.

The Supreme Court in a recent judgment has held that a Gárda may now stop a vehicle, even where he or she does not have a reasonable suspicion of a crime and may validly use evidence against the motorist should they find it. This marks a new and uncertain departure for Irish motorists.

There are many other road traffic prosecutions which can take place. Prosecutions for speeding offences are very frequent in District Courts all over the country. There are also frequent summons for failure to have vehicles taxed or for failure to have tax discs displayed.

Prosecutions under the Road Traffic Acts for failure to maintain vehicles to a proper standard are also frequent. In many cases repeat offenders under the Road Traffic Acts can risk being disqualified from driving. This in turn can result in loss of employment where vehicles are essential in the course of employment. The value of a Solicitor being retained when a person receives summons under the Road Traffic Acts is that he or she can advise as to whether the prosecution can be contested or admitted.

Where a District Court prosecution under the Road Traffic Acts is being contested the Solicitor will be familiar from a number of years of experience as to the relevant legal considerations. The ultimate sanctions resulting from conviction is a road traffic prosecution can be lessened considerably as a result of a successful presentation by your Solicitor of your case in Court.

Careless Driving

This offence constitutes driving a vehicle in a public place without due care and attention. This is a lesser offence to that of dangerous driving and carries a penalty of a fine not exceeding £350.00 and/or imprisonment of up to three months.

Driving Without Due Care and Attention

It is an offence for a person to drive a vehicle in a public place without reasonable consideration for other persons using that place. This again is a lesser offence than careless driving. Sometimes when a driver makes an error of judgment he may be convicted of driving without due care and attention. The penalty for conviction on the first offence is a fine of up to £150.00 and subsequent offences the fine is up to £350.00 and/or three months imprisonment.

9 DEFAMATION

Talk is said to be cheap. To any practising lawyer be it solicitor or barrister talk, in the form of advice, plays a major part in their livelihood. To the layperson, therefore, the value of talk, written or spoken, should not be underestimated as to what it can achieve, or as to the damage it can cause when improperly applied. The function of the Irish law of defamation is to protect against the wrongs of libel and slander.

Libel

Libel is the permanent form of slander. Libel could be in writing, broadcast on tv or radio or in some other permanent form. Words spoken on a live T.V. broadcast if defamatory would be classed as libel, as well as slander, as they are capable of being recorded and therefore turned into a permanent form. Similarly newspaper articles, magazines, books, if they damage the reputation of others unjustly may be considered libellous and the persons involved in the creation, publishing, distribution and resale of these may be held liable to account for them in Court by the offended person.

Slander
Slander on the other hand is spoken only. For a libel or slander to be actionable the words complained of, must be read or heard by

a third party. No action will arise against a person who speaks slanderous words to the plaintiff only and in private. But if a by-passer were to hear these words then technically a case could be made and the slanderer sued in Court.

The big difference between libel and slander as far as the layperson is concerned is one of damage (not damages!) or injury. For a slander (spoken words only) to be capable of an action in court, the plaintiff or person making the complaint, would have to prove financial loss as a result — but with four exceptions. For a libel to succeed (i.e in writing or in some permanent form) the plaintiff need only show the words were libellous in a legal sense, and the defendant has no legally acceptable excuse for publishing or broadcasting them. Damage or injury measured in financial loss need not be proved. This is of great annoyance to the media and they campaign vigorously to have this long established law changed.

How to recognise a defamation

There is (like a lot of our law) no definite way or "easy to use" formula to be applied while recognising defamation. The best way (and it is the way the courts use) is to go back over famous legal causes and pick from them the definitions used by judges down through the years. Here are some of the more famous ones.

A defamation arises when
1.   A statement lowers the person in the eyes of society generally.
2.   or "in the eyes of the average thinking man".

3. or "tends to hold that person up to hatred ridicule or contempt".
4. or "causes that person to be shunned or avoided".

The standard of the "reasonable man" is used to judge whether a statement is defamatory or not.

Why have any law of defamation?

Article 40.3.2 of the Irish Constitution. "The State guarantees… to protect from unjust attack, and in the case of injustice done, vindicate the… good name… of every citizen".

Another example from a judicial remark, (i.e. common or judge made law) "Speaking generally the law of this land recognises in every man the right to have the estimation in which he stands in the opinion of others unaffected by false statements to his discredit; and if the false statements are made without lawful excuse, and damage results to the person of whom they are made, he has a right of action". So said the eminent judge Cave J, in the case of Scott v. Samson in 1882.

This is the present state of Irish law now and for the foreseeable future. Of course, if a person is not of good reputation with regard to the words complained of, they will probably have no case.

The Extent of Defamation

Many people need to hear or read a defamatory remark before the plaintiff has a case. A rule of thumb here is the more people that hear or read the words complained of, the greater damages will be.

The number of plaintiffs must, however, be limited, i.e. a section of society for example a local club, or the residents of a village or town, or even some of them. It is useful to know the extent of the defamation in order to calculate the damages which a plaintiff could receive. One Judge actually held that should one person (i.e. a third party) receive the defamatory remarks this would be good enough for a case to succeed.

When assessing a defamatory remark there is however a line over which a court will not pass. Mere vulgar abuse is not defamatory. Such comments would not be actionable. It is unlikely that were such comments in writing, they would be so protected.

Some claims may be struck out as frivolous or vexations, or a court might find that a statement was mere humour and therefore not defamatory. It is possible, however, that some forms of satire are increasingly defamatory.

Innuendo

It is important to realise that the meaning of words could cast a broader net to catch an unwary defamer than one might expect. Should the plaintiff fail to succeed on the "ordinary and natural" meaning of the words he or she might well succeed on the innuendo.

An innuendo occurs where a statement which is at first glance innocent, may later be shown to have a different meaning altogether from its initial context. This is a complex and misleading area of law because as one strays from the 'ordinary and natural' meaning of words, things become less clear.

(Briefly, extrinsic facts must be proved in order to change an inference into a legal innuendo).

Where more than one innuendo is defamatory, there is a separate action for each. This means that a plaintiff may have more than one case against the defamer and his or her assistants based on the same set of words. This is therefore the cause of a multiplicity of actions.

Identity of the Plaintiff

The offended person must establish this. Examples are the best way of explaining identity and innuendo.

An account of a bigamy trial was published in a newspaper involving a Harold Newstead, a thirty year old Cumberwell man. It was a true report of a trial but not of a thirty year old hairdresser of the same name from Cumberwell. A court held that, reasonable persons would take the "innocent" Harold Newstead as the person involved in the trial and allowed him to successfully sue the newspaper.

Indirect identification may also satisfy. A photograph of "Mr. C. a racehorse owner and Miss X, whose engagement has been announced", was printed in the daily newspapers. The plaintiff was Mr C's wife. She was not mentioned in the paper as the photograph showed her to be an immoral woman who has merely lived with Mr C. without being married to him.

The number of people who are defamed may influence whether an action can succeed. If I said "all lawyers are thieves", no lawyer could bring an action against me, unless I indicated a particular lawyer. If however I said, "all lawyers in town X are thieves" (there being only six lawyers in that town) then each could bring an action against me. The rule therefore is, if the number of people of a certain type , or group, is small enough, so that the individuals can be reasonably identified, then it will give grounds for an action.

Words must be issued to a third party

This is required by law to establish defamation. It can be written or verbal as mentioned, a defamation cannot be 'published' to a plaintiff alone and still give grounds for an action.

Therefore the sending of a sealed letter to a plaintiff alone containing a libel cannot be defamation. If, on the other hand a libel is sent to a person on the back of a post card it will constitute a defamation. The logic being that the postman has a chance to read the 'words complained of'.

A similar comparison is where a defendant talks loudly, but in private to a plaintiff uttering defamatory words. It is reasonable to assume some third party will hear them. Alternatively leaving libellous comments written on paper where they may be casually read by passers-by is defamatory by presumption.

Defamation Inside Marriage

A communication between spouses is not publication but is shielded by "the cloak of privilege". This is partly based on the social regard for the institution of marriage and partly on the fact that it would make society intolerable if statements between husbands and wives could support defamation actions.

However, when a third party makes a defamatory comment to one spouse concerning the other it provides a reason for a defamation action. There is no law at the moment as to the position of persons living together or persons whose marriage is not recognised in the State.

Innocent Carriers

Strictly speaking every person who repeats a libel or carries it is a potential defendant and can be sued.

To avoid liability, an innocent carrier (e.g. magazine or newspaper wholesaler etc) must prove (i.e. he or she is presumed "guilty"):

a) They had no knowledge of the libel contained in the material distributed.

b) They were not alerted from the surrounding circumstances that libellous matter was contained within (an objective test).

c) That he/she was not negligent on his/her part in failing to know that it contained a libel.

In a case reported in the English courts in the 1970's a plaintiff succeeded in issuing seventy four writs against thirty seven wholesale and retail outlets. Assuming success against even half of these defendants the damages he could have received, when added together (they were all separate actions), would have been quite large. In effect, many of the distributors agreed as a settlement not to carry the offending publication.

Slander

Libel when published is actionable once the person of whom the 'words complained of' is identified. Loss to that person does not have to be proved.

Slander does require the proof of financial loss except on four very specific occasions. When these arise the plaintiff may proceed with an action without proof of financial loss.

The Exceptions

1   Saying about someone that they committed a crime punishable by a prison sentence.
2   Saying someone has a contagious disease which is likely to cause others to avoid the plaintiff.
3   Saying words which tend to cause injury to the plaintiffs office, profession, calling, trade or business.
4.   Saying words which suggest unchastity or adultery on a woman or a girl.

So, anyone who openly makes a false accusation that a person has stolen goods would be liable in defamation. Similarly saying someone has A.I.D.S. when it is untrue leaves one open to a defamation action.

Injury to a trade, business profession etc, requires two points to be proved by the plaintiff to make the case actionable without proof of financial loss as a result of the offending words.

1.   They were spoken of the person in his or her trade, profession etc.
2.   That were likely to cause injury in the area, i.e. financial loss.

Thus, a false statement about a solicitor that "He brought an action in the Circuit Court rather than the District Court so he could get more costs for himself" was held to be likely to damage the plaintiff's reputation as a Solicitor. The position here is where the words might tend to disparage him in his trade or profession need only be proved.

Again, for all other slanders special damage must be proved.

The Court

Actions for libel and slander are heard before a Judge alone in the Circuit Court and in the High Court he/she sits with a Jury. It is for the Judge to decide as a matter of law whether the statement being complained of is reasonably capable of bearing the defamatory meaning alleged by the Plaintiff. The case is withheld from the Jury if the Judge is not satisfied. However if the Judge decides that the words are capable of such a defamatory meaning then it is put to the Jury to decide whether those words have in fact the defamatory meaning complained of. There are a number of Defences which may be pleaded by a Defendant in a defamation action and these are dealt with later.

The Loss

It is not enough to succeed on loss of reputation alone. Special damage must be measured in money for moneys worth. So, the loss of a material benefit (such as accommodation, allowance etc) of hospitality is special damage. The loss of a measurable business advantage is allowable, as also is the loss of a client.
Defences

There are general and specific devices allowed by law in cases where defamation proceedings are brought against a person. Lapse of time is always a good defence where applicable. Consent to the statement in question may also be raised as a defence.

More specifically, there are five defences in defamation action which are worth noting.

Justification

Also known as the defence of truth. The "words complained of" must be substantially true for the defence to succeed. A railway company printed a true notice that a passenger had travelled unlawfully and was fined £1 and sentenced to three weeks in default of this where in fact he was sentenced to two weeks, was held by a court not to be grounds to succeed. Where a defamation is partially true the defence may be effective against the whole statement.

It may be dangerous to plead justification as a failure to persuade a Court may lead to aggravated damages being awarded against the defendant.

Fair Comment

If the statement is in the area of "public interest" this defence may be effective. It must not be a personal attack but a remark on the plaintiff's public work. It must also be objectively 'fair'. If malice is the motivation behind the comment it will destroy this defence.

Absolute Privilege

Where there is national importance the law allows freedom to communicate information. All reports of the Oireachtas and the President in office are also covered. Parliamentary committees and witnesses to these are also covered. It is also generally noted that communication between solicitors is absolutely privileged. Where absolutely privilege is established statements contained therein are not actionable under any circumstances.

Qualified Privilege

Where a person acts in good faith and without an improper motive, he or she may be protected even where a statement is untrue and defamatory. Where malice can be shown by the plaintiff, however, this will destroy this defence. For qualified privilege to apply it must be established that there was a legal or moral duty to make it on the one hand and a corresponding interest to receive it on the other. The absence of malice must also be proved.

Malice

This can be described in several ways such as

a   Wrong and improper motive, or,

b   Lack of good faith, or,

c   In order to injure the complainant.

In some cases spite or ill will may constitute malice or in others a reckless disregard for the truth might be enough. It depends on the defendant's motivation.

Apology

These are often printed in the media or announced on the radio or television. If the apology is speedy and sincere, it will help greatly to reduce the damages awarded. It is not, however, a defence as such. The apology must be shown to have been a genuine apology in order to be taken into account by the Court in assessing damages.

Compensation

This comes in the form of damages. An injunction may also be awarded as an alternative i.e. the court can order the publication to cease circulation.

Damages take the form of four different types and may be added together, to come up with a final figure. These are:

1   Compensatory Damages

These are not confined to the financial loss but are based on what is 'reasonable' as far as money can do, to restore the plaintiff to the position he or she enjoyed before the defamation.

2   Nominal Damages

If, for example there was a defamation found by a court but the damage was slight, the plaintiff could be awarded a small sum as compensation.

3   Contemptuous Damages

4   Punitive Damages

These may be awarded where for example, a defendant faced with the truth of his or her misdeeds refused to apologise and uses court time in an inappropriate way. In other words blatant misbehaviour.

Punitive damages may be applied by a court to teach a defendant that defamation does not pay, to deter him or her and to dissuade others.

In Ireland there is no limit to the amount of damages which may be awarded against a defendant in the High Court.

Conclusion

The reader may rightly get the impression that defamation when it occurs, can be real trouble for the person who writes, publishes, carries or otherwise repeats it. In a successful action a plaintiff often has multiple actions in which should he or she succeed, the sums in compensation can be large.

A criticism of the system is its in-built partiality to those who stand objectively to loose the most in our s1ociety, i.e. rich and famous. These people tend to get higher compensation awards. One must also ask the question, 'does their reputation suffer as a result of the defamatory words of the defendants?

The defamation laws are part of nineteenth century thought and values which, by their construction, give maximum twentieth Century effect to this a modern-day civil, constitutional, or political right, the right to a good name.

10 CRIME

Introduction.

There are two types of law: Civil Law, some of which is outlined in the chapters of this book, occupies the vast majority of the time of the legal professional. Criminal Law, on the other hand, is only a minor part by comparison. Many barristers and solicitors never involve themselves in criminal law. It is considered by many to be the 'poor relation' in terms of fees or income, but a Solicitor or Barrister with a good criminal practice can make a reasonable living from it.

What is Criminal Law?

Criminal law is a set of rules and principles which, if broken, result in a prosecution by the Gardaí or the Director of Public Prosecutions. These rules are the thresholds which, if crossed, offend against society as well as the victim. As the State by its laws guarantees to "vindicate the personal rights of the citizen" (Article 40.3.1° of the Constitution) it will impose the prosecutions available to it through the criminal law.

It is important for every citizen to acquaint themselves with the rules or laws of society. Ignorance of these is no excuse. Most Irish people are fortunate to have a reasonable grasp of what is morally right and wrong. This by and large is consistent with what the criminal law expects of us all. But in places they may not correspond exactly. Similarly, the criminal law, although crude in its application, (for example jail sentences are a pretty rough form of justice even in this day and age), can be finely tuned. This type of "fine tuning" is often outside the average lay person's complete understanding.

Criminal law can be broken down into two types of offences. These are real criminal offences and regulatory offences.

Regulatory Offences

These are the types of offences that many people may commit every day.

They include illegal parking, speeding, littering, breach of the licensing laws and many more. (The law Reform Commission of Canada in a recent report counted up to 35,000 regulatory offences on the statute books of that country). These offences however, are necessary to ensure an ordered society. Generally speaking, once a person has committed a regulatory offence they are liable to pay a fine, subject to a prosecution in the District Court.

Criminal Offences

These are what most people consider to be crime: murder, manslaughter, rape, burglary, larceny, assault and battery, everyone recognises these as crimes. Simple trespassing, even though a sign says "Trespassers will be Prosecuted" is not a crime. It is a civil wrong and is therefore not punishable by the State. (A trespasser could, however, be injuncted and ordered to pay damages by the Circuit Court should the occupier of that land choose to pursue the matter).

If a member of the Gardaí has reasonable grounds to believe that a person has committed a crime he or she will bring a prosecution against this person in their own name. An ordinary citizen may do likewise by the "laying of an information". This is known as the "common informer" method and applies to less serious crimes. In more serious situations the DPP will receive the reports, statements etc of witnesses in a file and prepare a prosecution against the alleged wrongdoer.

Two principles guide the persecutor in this:-

The presumption of non criminality. This means that if a crime is not listed as a crime a prosecution cannot be brought against the person.

The presumption of innocence. This means that everyone is presumed innocent until the state (Gardaí or DPP) prove, beyond reasonable doubt, that they are guilty.

"Beyond Reasonable Doubt"

In the District Court a judge sits alone. When he tries cases of a criminal nature he performs the dual function of deciding on the legality of the proceedings and deciding on the facts of the case, otherwise the function of the jury. In the Circuit Court the judge sits with a jury. The judge decides on the law and the jury decides on the facts.

The criminal process involves a very high standard of proof. Compare this to a civil proceedings to help understand what this means. In a civil case e.g. where a person sues someone for damages the case is decided on the balance of probabilities. This could be compared to an even decision. If the probability is more than fifty per cent that the person is liable, that person will be fixed with damages, and will have to pay compensation.

In criminal proceedings the standard of proof is much higher. Mere probability is insufficient. It must be definitively proved beyond "all reasonable doubt" that the person is guilty. If the State or Prosecutor cannot prove this the defending Solicitor or Barrister will ask for a "direction" i.e. that the case proceed no further and the charges dropped.

Evidence

Sometimes it is possible to have evidence suppressed or rendered inadmissible. If it is withheld from the Court the defence may then ask for a direct and the prosecution may have to be dropped.

Evidence can be taken completely out or can be admitted. Often when it is admitted it is accompanied by a warning from the judge to the jury to the effect that it is dangerous and grave to convict the accused on such evidence without thoughtful and deep consideration given to the facts.

Examples of evidence in general are not alone confined to the smoking gun or the bloody knife but come in the form of statements of witnesses either written or oral. The witnesses can be lay observers or experts.

Some examples of evidence which may require a warning to the jury or which, if improperly obtained may be disallowed and therefore not admitted are:-

Confessions

A confession is a statement by the accused admitting the acts alleged. It may be in writing even though the exact words of the accused need not be used. Once it is signed by him or her it can be used as evidence. A confession, once made to a "person in authority" can also be repeated by that person under oath and used in evidence. A person in authority could be a member of the Gardaí, Customs or Prison Service for example. So to admit to speeding when asked by a Gárda could be a confession.

If however a confession is not given under free will or if coercion or pressure is used, that could render the confession inadmissible. Words used to induce confessions like "it will be easier on you if you confess" or "do I have to go to your house and find out who did do it" have been held, when used by members of the Gardaí, to be inducements rendering the confessions given on foot of such as inadmissible.

The right to silence, as a constitutional right of every accused person, is used to guard us against ourselves from saying something which could be a confession.

Evidence Unconstitutionally Obtained

The courts are very watchful that the power of the State does not overstep its authority. They will punish the police authority when the rights of the citizen are abused by the misuse of such power, by disallowing such evidence. There are exceptions to this rule however and occur in the following circumstances.

1. Consent; A person may consent to a search and seizure operation by the Gardaí etc.
2. The power may exist under certain statutes to seize goods and submit them in evidence. These are, however, limited.
3. A person can be lawfully searched where it is necessary to protect the arresting officer.
4. A search on a lawful and properly signed search warrant.

A mere illegal act on behalf of the Gardaí etc if unintentional, and if once off, or a technical breach of a search warrant, e.g. wrong address, does not automatically strike down a search warrant. However if it is abusive of the person's constitutional rights in a way that seems to be an ongoing policy by the Gardaí or other arresting persons, it will be deemed inadmissible, and the case may well fail in court for the want of it.

Children

A child under the age of seven years cannot be capable of a criminal act. A child aged between 7 and 14 years of age can be found guilty but is presumed to be incapable unless they can be shown to have clear knowledge of the wrongfulness of their act. A child may however act as a "common informer" in a criminal matter.

Aiders and Abettors

Any person who aids, assists, advises, or gives equipment for use in a crime will be liable for prosecution and, if found guilty, liable to the same sentence as though they carried out the crime. This includes, receiving stolen goods with knowledge.

Time Limits

In minor offences, if the making of a complaint does not happen within 6 months of the wrongful act having been committed, it will become barred from further proceedings.

There is no time limit for serious offences unless a particular statute says so.

In particular courts are reluctant to convict wrongdoers who are brought to trial a long time after they are alleged to have committed the crime. This is because of the age of evidence. In particular the evidence of eye witnesses due to the failing capacity of the average person's memory. One can take it as a rule of thumb that if it goes over three years or more the likelihood of a conviction becomes very remote in many cases. However there have been cases of successful prosecutions of sexual offences against children which took place many years previously.

Arrest

Gardaí have powers of arrest under various Acts and at common law. An arrest is the term used for a person's apprehension for the purpose of bringing· that person before a Court. Under the common law a Garda may arrest a person he or she sees committing one of a number of felonies, breaches of the peace, assaults or obstruction of Gardaí in the execution of their duty.

Further powers of arrest are granted under various pieces of legislation. Among these are offences regarding robbery; larceny; possession of fire arms; contravention of barring orders; offences under the Liquor Licensing Laws; offences of malicious damage to property; offences involving crimes under Offences Against the State Act, 1939, i.e. membership of an illegal organisation; murder; arson; kidnapping and various offences against the Road Traffic Acts.

There are specific regulations in respect of persons held in custody. These are governed by the Criminal Justice Act, 1984 (Treatment of Persons in Custody in Garda Siochána Stations) Regulations, 1987. A custody record must be kept in respect of each person held in custody and this must include such information as the date, time and place of arrest, the reason for the arrest, the identity of the person arrested, the identity of the Garda who made the arrest, details of visits made to the person in custody, and such records must be kept for a minimum period.

An arrested person must be informed of certain information including the alleged offence for which he or she has been arrested, the person's entitlement to consult a Solicitor and if under seventeen years of age that a parent, guardian or spouse will be notified of the arrest and asked to attend the Garda Station.

A copy of the charge sheet containing particulars of the offence must be given to the person. There is a specific legislation in relation to the period of detention depending upon the offence for which the person has been arrested. There are also regulations in relation to the conditions under which a person is held in custody. Medical treatment must be provided if a person specifically requests this because of some particular medical condition from which the person suffers.

Detained Persons Right to a Solicitor

A person detained by the Gárda Síochána has a right to reasonable access to his legal advisers. A refusal to him or her in this regard renders the detention illegal and any statement made will not be admissible. (An illegal detention has serious consequences for the detaining officer. He or she may then be liable to be sued for damages by the detained person.) Reasonable in this context means having regard to all the circumstances of each individual case particularly as to the time at which access is required and the availability of the legal adviser sought.

The person detained must be given the opportunity to such a consultation out the hearing of members of the Gárda Síochána. The person themselves may ask for a Solicitor, or an interested bone fide party (such as a husband or wife etc) may ask for them. A person must be granted access to a Solicitor within a reasonable time of their requesting to do so. For example where an accused's Solicitor was denied access to his client it was held to be an illegal detention by a Court.

A person under the age of seventeen must be given an opportunity to have a parent or guardian present during questioning.

Legal Aid in Criminal Cases.

If a person is charged with an offence which is likely to impose a jail sentence if guilty, the District Court Judge should inform the defendant to his right to legal aid. Where the circumstances so demand, in the case of an unemployed person of no means it is necessary for the Judge to grant a certificate of legal aid.

Basic Trial Procedure

The giving of evidence in court is central to our criminal justice system. In Ireland we have an adversarial system of court practice, with the judge an impartial evaluator in a contest between the prosecution and defence.

The steps in a case are as follows:

The court clerk calls out the name of the case. For example the DPP vs. Jones, or in the common informer mode, Murphy v. Jones. This is pronounced "Murphy and Jones". Murphy in this imaginary case is the name of the person who lays the complaint, and is usually a Gárda.

The prosecutor states the charge. The accused is then questioned by the Judge as to their defence, if they have a Solicitor and if not as to their eligibility for legal aid. If they have a Solicitor and wish to plead not guilty the person laying the complaint takes the witness box and is sworn in. If it is a citizen who lays the complaint and are present in Court they would take the stand and be sworn in. If the case is taken by the DPP the accused person (if the charge is serious) is given the option of summary trial there and then or trial by jury at Circuit Court level. The examination-in-chief (i.e. examination by the prosecutor) then occurs. The witness is asked to state all the relevant facts concerning the complaint. The prosecutor may not ask leading questions, but may do so in order to identify persons or things in Court. A leading question is usually answered by a 'yes' or 'no'

Cross-examination is then carried by the defendant solicitor. Cross-examination has been described as "the most effective weapon yet devised to test truth". During this a defendant's

Solicitor can ask any leading question. (However exceptions exist as to the defendants previous offences and the witnesses relationship to the accused). The questions asked by the defendant's Solicitor may be of a general nature but not to such an extent that he or she indulges in "fishing" for information.

After this the prosecution may re-examine the witness as to matters which have arisen in the course of cross examination.

Hostile Witnesses

This is a person who is not inclined to tell the truth to the person who has called him. The Judge decides if a person can be treated as a hostile witness. If a witness is deemed hostile by the Judge the examination-in-chief may then take the form of a cross-examination.

An unfavourable witness is not a hostile witness. This is a witness who is called to prove a particular fact but fails to do so.

The Accused Person

The accused person cannot be called to give evidence in favour of his own prosecution. Where there is more than one defendant. They cannot testify or give evidence against each other. There are however some exceptions to this general rule.

For example

a)   An accused person once found guilty and sentenced can give evidence against the other

b)   If the charges are dropped against one accused, they may then give evidence against the other. Similarly, if the accused is acquitted (this means that the State's case has failed), they can then give evidence against the other.

A spouse cannot normally be compelled to give evidence, or testify, against the other spouse except in exceptional cases such as child abuse situations.

"The Shield"

An accused person when they take the stand to give evidence put themselves in a dangerous position. They are obliged to answer the questions asked in a truthful manner. The law recognises this and attempts to prevent such persons, in the interests of fairness, from self incrimination. This is the "shield". During the giving of evidence therefore an accused cannot be asked about

a)   his or her other offences or previous convictions

b)   or about his or her bad character

unless such evidence is admitted by the court in the examination-in-chief, or unless he or she has thrown their "shield" away by putting their own character before the Court to consider, or by casting imputations on the character of the prosecution, or by giving evidence against another accused person who is up on the same charge.

An example of casting imputations on the prosecution could be accusations of an unfounded nature on a prosecuting Gárda which suggest that that Gárda did not act properly in the course of his or her duty, e.g. an accused might say "He set me up".

Up to this point the Judge and jury are all formally ignorant of the accused's previous history and character etc. If the shield is lost, evidence may then be entered regarding these to make the prosecution's case more favourable.

Assault

An assault constitutes an unlawful and violent attack on another person. There are a number of different assaults including common assault, assault occasioning actual bodily harm and assault causing grievous bodily harm. The penalties in each case are quite different. The maximum penalty for common assault is six months imprisonment and/or a £50.00 fine on conviction in the District Court or one year's imprisonment if dealt with in the Circuit Court. On summary conviction in the District Court the maximum penalty for assault occasioning actual bodily harm is one year's imprisonment but on indictment in the Circuit Court the penalty is up to five year's imprisonment. Assault causing grievous bodily harm carries a penalty of up to five year's imprisonment.

Murder

Murder is the unlawful and intentional taking of another person's life. The "unlawful" taking of another person's life means doing so without any lawful justification. Either expressed or implied intention must be proved. It must be proved that it was intended to kill or to cause serious injury. There is express intention where the accused states that he is going to kill his victim and does so. Intention can also be implied in a case where the facts disclose that such intention existed. There is a presumption of innocence in cases of children under seven years of age. Between the age of seven and fourteen years it must be shown that a child knew that what he or she was doing was wrong.

The mandatory penalty for murder is life imprisonment.

Manslaughter

Manslaughter is the unlawful taking of another person's life without full intention (malice aforethought). Manslaughter is distinguished from murder when it is proved that there is no prior intention to kill, for example where a person temporarily looses control and kills another in the heat of the moment. The plea of "provocation" is frequently made. This involves proving that the victim either said something or did some act which seriously provoked the accused. If a plea of provocation is accepted this may result in a charge of murder being reduced to manslaughter. A person may be found guilty of man-slaughter resulting from dangerous driving. (see chapter on Road Traffic Law).

Larceny

Larceny is defined as taking without the consent of the owner of anything which is capable of being stolen with the intention of permanently depriving the owner of it. Depending on the value of the property stolen a charge of larceny may be heard in the District Court. However, more serious cases are dealt with in the Circuit Criminal Court.

Robbery

Robbery is the offence of stealing where force is used. Attempted robbery is also an offence. A conviction can carry a penalty of up to imprisonment for life.

Burglary

This involves illegally entering a building with the intention of stealing or attempting to steal or causing unlawful damage to the building or causing bodily harm. This carries a penalty of up to fourteen years imprisonment.

Aggravated Burglary

Where an offensive weapon is used at the time a burglary is carried out the offence involved is known as aggravated burglary. There is a long list of offensive weapons including fire arms, knives and other weapons including imitation weapons. Conviction for aggravated burglary may carry a penalty of imprisonment for life.

Sentencing

Often the reason for public outcry, people generally do not have a full understanding of this most sensitive of areas.
There are several reasons for sentencing.

1. To punish the criminal.
2. To make an example of them to other "would be" criminals, i.e. to deter them.
3. To remove them from society at large.
4. To provide a revenge for the victim and for society at large.
5. To rehabilitate the offender.

Fixed Sentences

There are not, nor can there be, fixed sentences, if courts are to render true justice. Every convicted person has different circumstances. For example, even though prior convictions are not normally allowed at trial, during sentencing the prosecution can read the accused person's record out in Court. Every guilty person will have a different record. Other circumstances will have to be taken into account such as the severity of the crime, the impact on the victim and the other personal circumstances of all involved whether directly or indirectly. All of these matters will be weighed by the Judge before he or she will apply their personal experience and pass sentence.

Training of Judges

There is no training for judges. They operate on a personal and collective experience. The variation in sentencing from one Judge to another has been commented upon. There are those who consider that Judges should attend training course so that more uniform and consistent sentences will result. There are many different views in relation to the entire subject of crime and punishment. It is considered by some that far more resources should be invested in the research of the origins of criminal activity and in particular the area of prevention. It is believed that the investment solely in additional prisons and additional policing together with changing the bail laws may not go far enough in eradicating the serious crime problem which currently exists.

Bail

Bail is the releasing from custody of a person subject to him or her turning up subsequently for his or her trial. A District Judge having heard a bail application can decide whether or not to grant bail. When deciding to grant bail the accused enters into a bond for a particular amount and signs a document known as recognisances. In most cases an independent surety or bails person is required. If the accused fails to attend at his trial then the amount of bail is forfeited. The Judge can also impose certain conditions regarding bail, e.g. reporting to a Police Station etc.

A referendum is due to take place on 28th November, 1996. A "yes" vote will bring about a limitation in the right to bail. It is the view of the Taoiseach, John Bruton, that tougher bail laws will bring about greater public safety. He believes that a "yes' vote is necessary because a small group use current bail laws to get back on the streets and to re-offend. Mr Bruton has stated that Ireland has the weakest bail laws in Europe and that it is time to tilt the balance of laws in favour of the victim. A Court, in his view, should be allowed take full account of previous convictions in deciding on bail and that changing the Constitution would target persistent criminals.

Soon we will know if the bail laws have in fact been changed and whether or not this coupled with the expansion in police resources and building of extra prisons will have the desired effect given the lack of resources being invested in research into this entire area.

Directory

Capital Taxes Division, Revenue Commissioners, Dublin Castle, Dublin 2. Telephone: 01-6792777. Fax: 01-6793261

Chief State Solicitor's Office, Dublin Castle, Dublin 2. Telephone: 01-4784333 Fax: 01-4784279

Commissioners of Charitable Donations and Bequests for Ireland, 12, Clare Street, Dublin 2. Telephone: 01-766095

Department of Enterprise and Employment, Kildare Street, Dublin 2. Telephone: 01-6614444.

Department of Equality and Law Reform, 43/49 Mespil Road, Dublin 4. Telephone: 01-6670344. Fax: 01-6670366.

Department of Justice, 72/76 St. Stephens Green, Dublin 2. Telephone: 01-6789711. Fax: 01-6615461.

Director of Consumer Affairs, Fourth Floor, Shelbourne House, Shelbourne Road, Dublin 4. Telephone: 01-6613399. Fax: 01-6606763.

Director of Public Prosecutions, 44-45 St. Stephens Green, Dublin 2. Telephone: 01-6789222. Fax: 01-6610915.

Employment Appeals Tribunal, Davitt House, 65A Adelaide Road, Dublin 2. Telephone: 01-6614444. Fax: 01-6769047.

Family Mediation Service (under the auspices of the Department of Equality and Law Reform) Irish Life Centre, Block 1, Floor 5, Lower Abbey Street, Dublin 1. Telephone: 01-8728227 or 01-8728708.

General Solicitor - for Minors and Wards of Court, Aras Ui Dhalaigh, Inns Quay, Dublin 7. Telephone: 01-8725555 ext. 231. Fax: 01-8722681.

Insurance Ombudsman of Ireland, 77, Merrion Square, Dublin 2. Telephone: 01-6620899. Fax: 01-6620890.

Land Registry, Central Office, Chancery Street, Dublin 7. Telephone: 01-8732233. Fax: 01-8733300.

Law Centres, See Local Directory for various Law Centres.

Law Reform Commission, Ardilaun Centre, 111, St. Stephens Green, Dublin 2. Telephone: 01-6715699. Fax: 01-6715316.

Law Society, Blackhall Place, Dublin 7. Telephone: 01-6710711.

Legal Aid Board, St. Stephens Green House, Earlsfort Terrace, Dublin 2. Telephone: 01-6615811. Fax: 01-6763426.

Marriage Conselling Service, 24, Grafton Street, Dublin 2. Telephone: 01-8720341.

Patents Office, 45, Merrion Square, Dublin 2. Telephone: 01-6614144. Fax: 01-6760416.

Probate Office, Four Courts, Dublin 7. Telephone: 01-8725555.
District Probate Registries: Contact County Registrar in nearest County Town.

Registrar of Friendly Societies, Ship Street Gate, Dublin Castle, Dublin 2. Telephone: 01-6614333. Fax: 01-6795226.

The Valuation Office, 6, Ely Place, Dublin 2. Telephone: 01-6763211. Fax: 01-6789646.

The Valuation Tribunal, First Floor, Ormonde House, Upper Ormonde Quay, Dublin 7. Telephone: 01-8728177. Fax: 01-8728060.

INDEX

The Four Courts